EXCHANGE RATE DETERMINATION AND CONTROL

The experiences with the Exchange Rate Mechanism in the European Union have highlighted the difficulties of exchange rate control.

Exchange Rate Determination and Control investigates the determinants of exchange rates and evaluates the main options for policy makers in limiting exchange rate fluctuations. The author draws on empirical evidence from the experiences of the G7 countries over the last two decades. From this it is possible to reach several conclusions. First, coordination of monetary policies is the best way to 'manage' exchange rates. Second, foreign exchange market intervention appears to be more effective within currency blocs like the European Monetary System than on the major exchange markets. Third, capital/foreign exchange controls become ineffective in the long term and should not be seen as critical to the stability of exchange rate systems.

Exchange Rate Determination and Control also provides empirical evidence supporting a unified theory of determination for the two main exchange rates, DM/dollar and yen/dollar.

Giorgio Radaelli, who has for many years worked in the City of London as a specialist on interest and exchange rate forecasting, is currently Director and Senior Economist with Lehman Brothers.

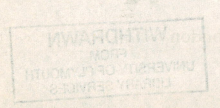

EXCHANGE RATE DETERMINATION AND CONTROL

Giorgio Radaelli

London and New York

First published 1995
by Routledge
11 New Fetter Lane, London EC4P 4EE

Simultaneously published in the USA and Canada
by Routledge
29 West 35th Street, New York, NY 10001

Typeset in Palatino by Solidus (Bristol) Limited
Printed and bound in Great Britain by
Mackays of Chatham PLC, Chatham, Kent

British Library Cataloguing in Publication Data
A catalogue record for this book is available from the British Library.

Library of Congress Cataloging in Publication Data
Radaelli, Giorgio, 1958–
Exchange rate determination and control/Giorgio Radaelli.
p. cm.
Includes bibliographical references and index.
1. Foreign exchange rates. 2. Foreign exchange rates – European
Economic Community countries. I. Title.
HG3851.R27 1994
332.4'56 – dc20   94–3981
                                                       CIP
ISBN 0–415–11103–X

To Tracey, Angela,
Benedetto and Nico

CONTENTS

Figures   ix
Tables   xi
Preface   xiii

INTRODUCTION   1

1 ERM STABILITY, CAPITAL CONTROLS
   AND FOREIGN EXCHANGE MARKET
   INTERVENTION   5
   Introduction   5
   The ERM performance and its determinants   6
   Foreign exchange market intervention within the ERM   14
   Conclusions   26
   Appendix 1   28
   Appendix 2   29

2 THE EFFECTIVENESS OF CAPITAL
   CONTROLS: AN EMPIRICAL ANALYSIS
   OF THE ERM   31
   Introduction   31
   Review of the issues   32
   The theoretical model   36
   Empirical results   40
   Conclusions   52
   Appendix 3   53

3 EXCHANGE RATE DETERMINATION:
   MONETARY OR PORTFOLIO-BALANCE
   EFFECTS?   55

CONTENTS

Introduction		55
The models considered		57
Empirical results		62
Conclusions		77
Appendix 4		80
4	ON THE EFFECTIVENESS OF FOREIGN EXCHANGE MARKET INTERVENTION	83
	Introduction	83
	Earlier evidence on intervention	83
	Direct tests on intervention	86
	Conclusions	89
CONCLUSIONS		91
Notes		93
References		99
Index		105

FIGURES

Figure 1	Domestic rate versus Eurofranc rate	11
Figure 2	Domestic rate versus Eurolira rate	11
Figure 3	France–Germany regression	20
Figure 4	France, capital controls parameter ϕ	45
Figure 5	France, actual versus no-controls case	46
Figure 6	Italy, capital controls parameter ϕ	49
Figure 7	Italy, actual versus no-controls case	50
Figure 8	Lira/DM, *ex post* risk premium	51
Figure 9	DM/$ model, parameters' evolution (cointegrating regression – relative wealth)	67
Figure 10	DM/$ model, parameters' evolution (cointegrating regression – real interest rates)	68
Figure 11	DM/$ model, actual versus equilibrium values	69
Figure 12	Plot of responses of DMDL	70
Figure 13	Plot of responses of GERI	71
Figure 14	Plot of responses of USRI	72
Figure 15	Yen/$ model, parameters' evolution (cointegrating regression – relative wealth)	75
Figure 16	Yen/$ model, parameters' evolution (cointegrating regression – interest rate spread)	76
Figure 17	Yen/$ model, actual versus equilibrium values	78
Figure 18	Plot of responses of YEDL	79

TABLES

Table 1	Correlation between overnight rates of interest	1
Table 2	Correlation between money supplies growth	2
Table 3	Exchange rate volatility	7
Table 4	Correlation between money supplies in ERM countries	9
Table 5	Correlation between interest rates and inflation in ERM countries	9
Table 6	Foreign exchange intervention by ERM countries	15
Table 7	Risk-premium equations, France–Germany	19
Table 8	Pre-ERM regressions	24
Table 9	Post-ERM inception regressions	25
Table 10	ML estimates of the capital control model	43
Table 11	Unit root tests on the variables considered	63
Table 12	Johansen maximum likelihood procedure (Germany)	65
Table 13	Estimated cointegrated vectors in Johansen estimation (Germany)	66
Table 14	Johansen maximum likelihood procedure (Japan)	74
Table 15	Estimated cointegrated vectors in Johansen estimation (Japan)	74
Table 16	Causality tests between intervention and exchange rates	88

PREFACE

This book investigates the macroeconomic determinants of exchange rates and evaluates the main levers available to policy makers for limiting exchange rate fluctuations. The book is empirical in nature and looks at various facets of the experience of the Group of Seven (G7) largest economies during the last two decades. The work is presented in four chapters. The first two look at exchange rates within the Exchange Rate Mechanism (ERM) of the European Monetary System (EMS) while the third turns to US dollar exchange rates. The fourth chapter presents evidence on sterilized foreign exchange market intervention on five main currencies.

Broadly speaking, policy makers have three tools with which to contain exchange rate volatility. First, coordination of (monetary) policies. Second, (sterilized) foreign exchange market intervention. Third, capital and foreign exchange controls. Policy coordination and controls lie at the extrema of the spectrum whereas sterilized intervention is often chosen by those policy makers who want to retain some monetary independence while minimizing the welfare losses caused by administrative controls.

The evidence presented in this book suggests the following:

1 Coordinated monetary policies, especially when affecting (real) interest rates, are almost always effective in steering exchange rates.
2 Sterilized foreign exchange market intervention may have some efficacy within currency blocs like that of the EMS area.
3 Capital and foreign exchange controls become ineffective in the long run.

4   Despite clear portfolio-balance influences on the DM/dollar and yen/dollar exchange rates, there is feeble evidence that foreign exchange intervention has had a significant impact on the main currencies outside the ERM.

My belief in the ineffectiveness of capital and foreign exchange controls led me to argue, in Chapters 1 and 2, that those controls were not the main source of stability of the ERM in the 1980s and that the ERM would outlive the process of financial liberalization culminating with the abolition of (French and Italian) controls in 1989–90. Indeed, the ERM ran smoothly for a couple of years after that, before falling prey to the speculators in September 1992 and August 1993. However, I would argue that the source of instability was the market awareness that the monetary policy of the German Bundesbank was out of tune with that of the other ERM members. Under such circumstances, realignments became inevitable and the ERM-wide reimposition of controls would, at best, have delayed the capitulation. Indeed, in the autumn of 1992 the Spanish authorities tried to defend the peseta by reintroducing controls but this proved fruitless as the Spanish unit was eventually devalued in November.

The research behind my conclusions has been influenced, at various stages, by the criticisms and comments of David Begg. Parts of the book have also benefited from comments by Niso Abuaf, Mike Artis, Vittorio Grilli, Gregory Hoelscher, Nick Robinson, Lakis Vouyoukas and Sykes Wilford. Naturally, none of them is responsible for any of the views expressed. Finally, I wish to thank Oxford University Press for their permission to reprint Chapter 1 whose material had previously appeared in *Private Behaviour and Government Policy in Interdependent Economies.*

September 1993

INTRODUCTION

The post-1973 period showed some unpleasant links between changes in monetary policies, real exchange rates and economic growth. These links have been documented, both theoretically and empirically, by analyses based on sticky-price monetary models of the exchange rate. The tendency towards more integrated capital markets has made those externalities all the more felt. As a result, closed-economy monetary policy fell progressively out of grace. Indeed, the last decade showed a trend towards less insular monetary policies,[1] revolving around attempts at curbing exchange rate volatility.

However, monetary coordination has been more significant among members of the ERM than the three major economies of the USA, Japan and Germany (G3). In fact, within the ERM area, the 1980s brought more highly correlated monetary growths and interest rates (see Tables 4 and 5), whilst among the G3 countries we note increased correlation for interest rates only (see Tables 1 and 2 below). This may reflect growing desynchronization in GDP

Table 1 Correlation between overnight rates of interest*

1973:1–1980:12 (1981:1–1991:12)	USA	Japan	Germany
USA		0.307 (0.395)	0.566 (0.631)
Japan			0.514 (0.735)

*Correlation coefficients are computed from monthly data

1

Table 2 Correlation between money supplies growth*

1973:1–1980:12 (1981:1–1991:12)	USA	Japan	Germany
USA		0.287 (−0.03)	0.310 (0.216)
Japan			0.714 (0.031)

*Correlation coefficients are computed from broad money (i.e. M2/M3) year-on-year growth rates

growth – the variable driving demand for money. Alternatively, it could reflect an increased use of unsterilized intervention – hence more diverging money supplies – as a complement to interest rate policy in checking exchange rate flexibility.

Perhaps the most important reason for policy coordination being more popular within Europe than at G3 level has been the ERM members' commitment towards building a low-inflation area. In fact, the policy coordination literature shows that ERM membership brings credibility advantages to countries which lack a reputation for low inflation when acting independently under flexible exchange rates.[2]

Another reason seems to be that the step change, between the 1970s and the 1980s, in financial liberalization has been more drastic in the main European economies than among the USA, Japan and Germany.

A consensus seems to have emerged amongst economists that a successful international monetary system would have, at a minimum, the following three characteristics:

1   It would have a nominal anchor resting on the commitment of the largest national economy to domestic price stability.
2   It would seek to facilitate international adjustment by encouraging countries to eliminate unsustainable external imbalances at source.
3   It would allow for different degrees of exchange rate flexibility across countries depending on the structural characteristics of the economies, the advantages of external discipline for monetary policy, and incentives to regional integration.

Combining 1 with 3 suggests that exchange rate commitments ought perhaps to be looser in the largest industrial countries than in smaller, more open economies – some of which may eventually even opt to join in regional currency areas.

From the above suggestions a question naturally follows: how will the (international monetary) system ensure that the main currencies, whose movements have the greatest impact on the rest of the world, are not subject to serious misalignments and/or excess volatility? In what follows I investigate the merits of different means for limiting exchange rate fluctuations.

Broadly speaking, policy makers have three tools with which to contain exchange rate volatility. First, coordination of policies, especially in the monetary arena. Second, greater recourse to sterilized foreign exchange intervention. Third, imposing administrative controls on cross-border capital flows. Policy coordination and capital controls lie at the extrema of the spectrum. Indeed, capital controls are, when effective, the ultimate means of preserving a monetary policy independent of foreign developments. Sterilized intervention can be seen, instead, as the choice of the policy maker who wants to retain some monetary independence without suffering the welfare loss caused by administrative controls on the international allocation of capital.

The main body of this book focuses on capital controls and foreign exchange intervention, especially within the ERM area. Issues of monetary coordination and G3 foreign exchange intervention are touched upon more tangentially, although the final chapter provides evidence on the efficacy of G3 intervention.

The first chapter looks at the role played by monetary coordination and foreign exchange intervention in delivering the ERM stability of the 1987–92 period. The results support the efficacy of both those tools against the long-standing belief that capital controls had been the key to the ERM performance.

The second chapter looks at the role of capital controls within the ERM in more detail. It provides further evidence in support of the view expressed in Chapter 1: that the role of capital controls should not be overrated. It seems, in fact, that intra-European capital controls ceased to bite since the mid-1980s.

The third chapter is an empirical examination of exchange rate determination models.[3] It concentrates on the G3 parities and follows an eclectic approach to test whether monetary or portfolio balance effects play a role in shaping those exchange rates. That type of analysis gives some clues on whether sterilized intervention can help to limit exchange rate flexibility.

The fourth chapter provides additional evidence on foreign exchange market intervention. It presents direct tests on whether sterilized intervention has had any systematic effect on the five main currencies over the period of floating exchange rates.

The final chapter distils the main conclusions of this book on how to limit exchange rate fluctuations.

1

ERM STABILITY, CAPITAL CONTROLS AND FOREIGN EXCHANGE MARKET INTERVENTION

INTRODUCTION

Since the mid-1980s, several studies have focused on two major aspects of the ERM. The first concerns the extent to which the system has actually produced welfare gains. Here, particular issues at stake are those related to the concepts of exchange rate volatility and misalignments. Therefore, it has been important to assess empirically to what degree the ERM has delivered greater exchange rate stability, both in nominal and real terms. Nominal exchange rate stability can be seen as a value in itself (worth paying for) as long as it boosts international trade and investment. An IMF study (1984) found no evidence of effects from nominal exchange rate volatility on world trade volumes. On the other hand, Cushman (1983) did find evidence of a negative effect from real exchange rate volatility to trade flows. Moreover, it is clear that exchange rate misalignments link in an undesirable way (via real exchange rate instability) one country's monetary policy with its international competitiveness, and hence output and employment (see Buiter and Miller (1981)). In sum, it seems that what is needed is real – not just nominal – exchange rate stability.

Whilst it can be shown that the ERM has actually fostered a higher degree of real exchange rate stability, it is unclear what are the 'costs' at which this has been achieved. This constitutes a second major aspect of the ERM debate to date.

In particular, have the costs been in terms of lost monetary

5

policy independence, capital controls, or foreign exchange market intervention, or a combination of the three? Until 1992, it appeared to be commonly held that costs had been mostly in the form of capital controls. (More recently, however, some commentators have put new emphasis on the costs due to losing the independence of national monetary policies.) In fact, some claimed that the ERM had stood together only thanks to administrative measures which distort the efficient allocation of resources.[1] Monetary integration was not credited with having played any role, let alone foreign exchange intervention. The main scope of this chapter is to reassess the relative importance of foreign exchange intervention as a determinant of ERM stability.

In the second section of this chapter, I start by discussing empirical evidence pertaining to the ERM performance, particularly in terms of exchange rate volatility. Then, I move to an analysis of the likely determinants of that performance. I present some results on monetary convergence in the ERM area after 1979 and put forward some arguments to reduce the relative importance of capital controls in determining the ERM stability seen between the late 1980s and early 1990s.

The third section discusses some empirical evidence suggesting that the relative importance of ERM foreign exchange intervention has been neglected. My evidence concerns a portfolio-balance channel affecting the risk premium on the major ERM currency markets and the compatibility of actual exchange rates' behaviour with a posited rule of thumb of (ERM) central banks' intervention.

The final section summarizes the results and conclusions.

THE ERM PERFORMANCE AND ITS DETERMINANTS

It is widely held that the major achievement of the ERM is to have favoured an unexperienced degree of exchange rate stability. This might be seen as a value in itself, particularly as long as dampened misalignments soften undesirable real exchange rate effects from domestic monetary policy to international competitiveness. It seems still to be proved that nominal exchange rate volatility *per se* has negative repercussions on international trade. Therefore, the

Table 3 Exchange rate volatility (coefficients of variation)[a]

	Nominal exchange rates		Real exchange rates	
	1973:1–1979:3	1979:4–1990:12	1973:1–1979:3	1979:4–1990:12
L/FF	0.0167	0.0039	0.0069	0.0047
L/DM	0.0284	0.0144	0.0059	0.0035
FF/DM	0.0132	0.0129	0.0093	0.0045
Y/$	0.0149	0.0096	0.0095	0.0099
Y/DM	0.0087	0.0189	0.0062	0.0129
£/$	0.0157	0.0237	0.0086	0.0182
£/DM	0.0238	0.0092	0.0062	0.0078
DM/$	0.0132	0.0189	0.0075	0.0189
ERM[b]	0.0194	0.0104	0.0074	0.0042
Non-ERM[c]	0.0153	0.0161	0.0076	0.0135

a Data are monthly averages. WPIs used to compute real exchange rates
b Average across: L/FF, L/DM, FF/DM
c Average across: Y/$, Y/DM, £/$, £/DM, DM/$
Source: International Financial Statistics

main merit of the ERM is likely to have been its contribution to greater real exchange rate stability.

Table 3 presents the coefficients of variation for some major nominal and real exchange rates, both before and during the ERM period (prior to sterling joining the system). Although analogous evidence has already been presented elsewhere, I think that a few further qualifications are not superfluous.

The picture emerging from Table 3 is one of increased nominal and real stability among ERM currencies during the ERM period. On the other hand, both nominal and real volatility have increased, after 1979, for the major non-ERM rates. In particular, 'average' real exchange rate volatility after 1979 decreased by more than 40 per cent within the ERM whilst it increased by nearly 80 per cent among non-ERM rates.

Qualitatively similar results are reported by, among others, Padoa Schioppa (1985), Wood (1986), Ungerer *et al.* (1986) and Rogoff (1985). Rogoff's results are of particular interest in that they refer to conditional variances (variances of forecasting errors) as opposed to unconditional variances, thus interpreting the concept of volatility in terms of forecastability.[2]

It has been argued (e.g. by Artis (1986)) that assessing volatility with respect to bilateral rates – as opposed to effective ones – is not appropriate in this context. The argument is that a member of the ERM could gain more stability for its currency *vis-à-vis* ERM members at the cost of increased volatility *vis-à-vis* non-member currencies. However, I would argue that a trade-off between intra-ERM and non-ERM stability is implied by the very fact that the system's original task was to achieve greater internal stability. This would naturally imply lower external stability as long as the ERM stands up as a single currency area facing other major ones. Greater external stability is out of the reach of the ERM and might be a task for a more general programme of international monetary reform which could or could not contemplate the existence of the ERM.

Therefore, I would restate the conclusion that the ERM has led to greater exchange rate stability. Although this can be seen as a value in itself, it is important to identify the means by which such a performance has been achieved. This may, in turn, allow one to gain a better perspective on how the system will (should) develop.

One major criticism against the ERM as it stood between 1985 and 1992 was that exchange rate stability had been warranted by capital controls rather than by convergence in economic policies. There is less consensus on whether (monetary) policies have been more convergent between member countries after 1979 than on the issue of relative exchange rate stability.

An unambiguous criterion by which to measure policy convergence (let alone cooperation) does not seem to be available yet. Therefore, in what follows I provide a rough idea of the extent to which the degree of convergence between ERM monetary policies has varied.

Tables 4 and 5 contain correlation coefficients (referring to Germany, France and Italy) between those variables which are most likely to be affected by monetary policy: monetary aggregates, interest rates and inflation rates. It turns out that the degree of correlation between all these variables has been higher during the ERM period than before.

However, these results should not lead one to claim that greater exchange rate stability has been unambiguously due to higher monetary convergence. First, as Artis (1986) points out, there is analogous evidence of increased monetary convergence also

Table 4 Correlation between money supplies[a] in ERM countries

	France		Italy		Germany	
	before ERM[b]	*after* ERM[c]	*before* ERM[b]	*after* ERM[c]	*before* ERM[b]	*after* ERM[c]
			M1			
France	–	–	-0.174	0.769	0.341	0.893
Italy	–	–	–	–	-0.457	0.637
			M2			
France	–	–	-0.078	0.80	0.33	0.371
Italy	–	–	–	–	-0.534	0.735

a Annual growth rates
b Monthly data, 1974:1–1979:3
c Monthly data, 1979:4–1990:12
Source: OECD, *Main Economic Indicators*, not seasonally adjusted data

Table 5 Correlation between interest rates and inflation[a] in ERM countries

	France		Italy		Germany	
	before ERM[b]	*after* ERM[c]	*before* ERM[b]	*after* ERM[c]	*before* ERM[b]	*after* ERM[c]
			Interest rates			
France	–	–	0.464	0.750	0.856	0.873
Italy	–	–	–	–	0.203	0.513
			Inflation rates			
France	–	–	0.997	0.999	0.574	0.995
Italy	–	–	–	–	0.574	0.993

a Consumer price index, year-on-year rate of growth, and three-month interest rates
b Monthly data, 1974:1–1979:3
c Monthly data, 1979:4–1990:12
Source: *International Financial Statistics*, and *Intline* data bank, Chase Econometrics

outside the ERM area, yet this has not been mirrored by greater exchange rate stability. Second, convergence may simply result from a process by which everyone 'puts their own house in order'; it need not result from adaptations of national monetary policies in recognition of international interdependence.[3]

Third, alternative attempts to detect an increased degree of

9

monetary convergence between Germany, France and Italy after 1979 failed. For instance, Rogoff (1985) cannot find evidence of a reduction in the conditional variance of real interest rate differentials between those three countries since 1979. Moreover, casual observation would spot periods in which the policy mix in these three countries was set to a large extent independently.[4] Fourth, taking a broader perspective, Bini Smaghi and Vona (1987) stressed that the real threat to ERM stability comes from a pronounced divergence in fiscal policy stance – leading to mounting trade imbalances – among Germany, France and Italy. Some would argue that this problem abated following the post-unification fiscal boost in Germany. However, the opposite is true for *Western* Germany whose fiscal stance actually became very tight between 1991 and 1993 (see Radaelli (1993)).

Therefore, I conclude there is no clear-cut evidence supporting the claim that economic policy coordination has been the only determinant of the ERM stability. There is, however, some evidence indicating that intra-ERM monetary policies have been more convergent in the 1980s than during the 1970s.

Consequently, some alternative determinants of the ERM stability should be looked for. The literature has commonly held that the main (only?) determinant of that stability has been capital controls.[5] The presumption here is that exchange rate variability can be reduced only by either coordinated policies or capital controls, or a combination of the two.

On the ERM, the picture would be one in which (a) the lack of policy coordination shifts the burden of stabilizing exchange rates onto domestic interest rates, (b) domestic authorities counter the consequent (and undesired) interest rate volatility by setting up capital controls which (c) shift the burden of absorbing ('jump') variable to offshore interest rates. Such a strategy would allow domestic authorities to maintain policy independence and exchange rate stability without paying the costs of greater domestic interest rate volatility.

That such a scheme diverts volatility from domestic to Euro-interest rates is shown by Figures 1 and 2 on French and Italian interest rates. In particular, in the proximity of realignments (whose dates are indicated by the R on the X-axis) the Eurolira and Eurofranc interest rates often carry the burden of compensating

10

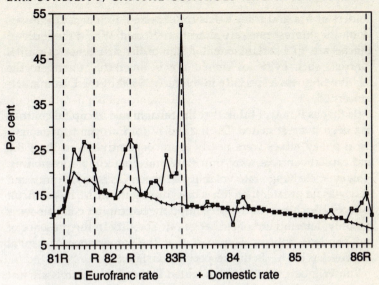

Figure 1 Domestic rate versus Eurofranc rate: one-month maturity, February 1981 to April 1986

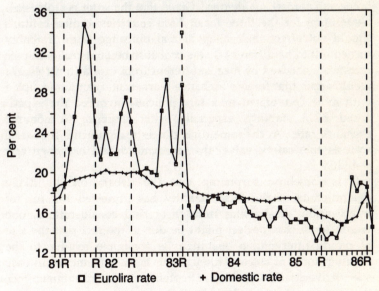

Figure 2 Domestic rate versus Eurolira rate: one-month maturity, February 1981 to April 1986

holders of lira and franc assets for expected exchange rate losses. Domestic interest rates are almost unaffected. Whilst these divergencies are, to a certain extent, a sign of the stringency of capital controls, such evidence should not be overrated owing to the relative thinness (especially in the early 1980s) of the Euromarkets concerned.

Be that as it may, I think that the relative role of capital controls has been overestimated. During the 1970s, European monetary-fiscal policy mixes were nearly as uncooperative as in the 1980s and capital controls were – in Italy and France – no less biting. However, exchange rate volatility between Germany, France and Italy was far greater than it has been during the ERM. It is difficult to reconcile this with the presumption that capital controls were the only determinant of exchange rate stability in the presence of independent policies. I suspect that the importance of capital controls has been – in this respect – overstated.

Van Wijnbergen (1985) highlighted that capital controls are just interventions in intertemporal trade. *Ceteris paribus* they are unlikely to affect the real exchange rate if expenditure patterns at home and abroad are identical. Given that the latter is a plausible assumption for the three major EMS countries, capital controls should not affect their bilateral real exchange rates. If reality turned out to be different it was probably because real exchange rates were checked by means different from capital controls. We would argue that foreign exchange market intervention (coupled with more convergent monetary policies) favoured the experienced ERM stability, especially with reference to nominal exchange rates. At the same time, timely realignments should be seen as the 'safety valve' that guaranteed real exchange rate stability.

It is somehow surprising that the debate on the likely determinants of the ERM stability has neglected the role of intervention. Abstracting from theoretical considerations, one reason for such a neglect might be due to the fact that the size of typical intervention operations is negligible relative to the existing stocks of assets. Although this is true at times of intense speculative attacks like those of September 1992 and summer 1993, that argument is weakened, during calmer periods, by the presence of ERM institutional arrangements explicitly boosting the funds available to member central banks for intervention.

The agreement of 13 March 1979 among EC central banks laying down the procedures specifies that 'interventions will be unlimited at the compulsory intervention rates' and that 'other interventions (those not at the margins) will be conducted in accordance with the ... guidelines adopted by the committee of governors ... or will be subject to consultations among all the participating central banks'. Moreover, 'when a currency crosses its threshold of divergence, this results in the presumption that the authorities concerned will correct this situation by adequate measures, including diversified intervention'. Thus (also) intra-marginal intervention appears to have a role in the management of the system.

The financing of ERM intervention is ensured by the Very Short-Term Financing Facility (VSTFF). This consists of mutual loans enabling each central bank to make its own currency available to others. The operations are in the form of spot sales/purchases of currencies against the crediting/debiting of ECU accounts held with the European Monetary Cooperation Fund. Such operations are automatically renewable at the debtor's request. Moreover, in the spring of 1985 a new scheme was set up for mobilizing ECU holdings whereby participating central banks can obtain dollars or ERM currencies through three-month swaps, without restrictions on the type of intervention involved. Thus it became possible to borrow currency for intramarginal intervention too.[6] Furthermore, the divergence threshold (*vis-à-vis* the ECU) mechanism ensures that the burden of intervention is more evenly split than in a Bretton Woods-like setting. This, of course, can be thought of as further boosting the role of routine, intra-marginal, intervention within the ERM framework.

Finally, the very fact that the participating countries are fairly homogeneous and commercially integrated ensures that they share real disturbances – particularly supply-side shocks. This should contribute to minimize the number of times in which it is optimal to realign,[7] and should also allow the policy makers to recognize promptly when exchange rate adjustments are called for. An example of asymmetric supply-side shock which would have required a realignment is Germany's reunification in 1991. However, the politicians decided to ignore policy advice that the

DM should be revalued, thus opening the way to the market-induced realignments of 1992 and 1993.

The next section discusses empirical evidence on the role of foreign exchange intervention within the ERM.

FOREIGN EXCHANGE MARKET INTERVENTION WITHIN THE ERM

As pointed out by Masera (1986), two types of intervention can be envisaged within the system:

1   *Symmetric* monetary base interventions, i.e. those entailing simultaneously opposite effects on the monetary base of both the country causing the intervention and the country whose currency is used.[8]
2   *Asymmetric* monetary base interventions, carried out by one central bank through Eurocurrency or domestic private banking assets in the other currency. Only the monetary base of the country which originates the intervention is affected in this case, unless the monetary authorities 'sterilize'.

Given that intramarginal intervention has, as we show below, been widely used, type 2 has probably been the most used scheme despite the fact that type 1 would theoretically have a stronger impact on the exchange rate.

There is evidence of an increased role for intervention after 1979. Galy (1984) estimates an exchange rate–interest rate–net foreign assets model for major ERM countries. He finds that the stability of parameters – before and after the inception of the ERM – cannot be rejected for the exchange rate equations only. In particular, the statistical significance of the parameters in the net foreign assets equation increases after 1979. The likely explanation for such a structural break is that, after 1979, ERM central banks intervened more aggressively in the foreign exchange market.

Additional evidence for the early 1980s is reported in Table 6. From our viewpoint, the most important implication of the data is that less than 15 per cent of total ERM interventions were carried out at the compulsory intervention limits.[9] The remaining intervention was intramarginal, in contrast with the *ex ante* perception of a modest role for intramarginal intervention (see Micossi (1985)).

Table 6 Foreign exchange intervention by ERM countries[a]

	1979[b]	1980	1981	1982	1983	1984	1985
US dollar (plus others)	23.6	27.5	42.6	39.3	32.5	23.2	25.0
EMS currencies							
at the limits	2.5	3.9	11.1	3.0	13.3	1.9	2.1
intramarginal	5.4	4.5	9.4	9.9	13.1	13.7	18.9
Recourse to VSTFF	3.3	2.5	9.0	2.3	5.4	1.8	–

a In billions of US dollars. Figures are the sum of purchases and sales
b March to December
Source: European Monetary Cooperation Fund (after Micossi (1985))

Such empirical regularity corroborates my previous arguments supporting the role of this type of intervention.

However, it is one thing to know that central banks intervened to an unexpected degree, and another to maintain that these interventions did affect ERM exchange rates. It is generally agreed that a necessary condition for sterilized intervention to be effective is one of the following:

1   that agents regard domestic and foreign securities as imperfect substitutes and they do not treat the securities held by authorities as being part of private sector portfolios;
2   that intervention affects expectations about the future course of monetary policy.[10]

Condition 1 is the most commonly tested of the two hypotheses and implies that a portfolio-balance model of exchange rate determination holds. The currency composition of asset supplies would be a key determinant of both the exchange rate and its risk premium. Although the latter might in principle be affected also by default risk, we rule out such a possibility, at least within the EMS area. (Admittedly, Italy's and Belgium's public debts of more than 100 per cent of GDP may cast some doubt on my assumption.) Naturally, the presence of capital controls makes domestic and foreign assets more likely to be imperfect substitutes. Therefore, only detection of a systematic risk-premium component independent of capital controls would give substantial support to the

15

effectiveness of foreign exchange market intervention carried out in the absence of controls.

It is customary to associate the idea of perfect asset substitutability with the monetary model of exchange rate determination. Such a model maintains, as one of its distinguishing assumptions, that *ex post* uncovered interest parity (UIP) holds on average.

Broadly speaking, there are two possible reasons for UIP not holding:

1   agents may not be rational;
2   agents, whilst being rational, may be risk-averse, thus demanding a risk premium in the presence of imperfectly substitutable domestic and foreign assets.

Two empirical strategies have been typically employed to detect a portfolio-balance channel capable of explaining the risk premium:

1   estimation of inverted bond demand (risk-premium) equations;
2   estimation of exchange rate quasi-reduced forms derived from the general portfolio-balance model.[11]

In our empirical analysis I follow strategy 1, thus considering the risk premium as systematic deviations from UIP. My exercise will involve – not unusually – the testing of a joint hypothesis concerning the formation of expectations and the presence of a (portfolio-balance-related) risk premium.

Typically, this kind of empirical work finds it difficult to explain systematic deviations from UIP. However, maintaining the risk-premium interpretation seems to be the only way to continue to believe that agents are rational in the face of deviations from UIP.

When domestic and foreign currency assets are perfect substitutes, i.e. there is no risk premium, expectations are rational and interest rate movements are not dampened by capital controls, the following holds:

$$(1 + i_t)/(1 + i_t^*) = E_t S_{t+1}/S_t \qquad (1)$$

where: i = domestic interest rate
i^* = foreign interest rate

S = units of domestic currency per unit of foreign currency

E_t = mathematical expectation (conditional on information available at time t) operator

Within the monetary model of exchange rate determination, domestic and foreign assets are perfect substitutes, i.e. there is no systematic risk premium, so that (1) holds on average. Conversely, the portfolio-balance model emphasizes imperfect asset substitutability and hence systematic deviations from (1).

Within a portfolio-balance model framework it is possible to derive (see Appendix 1) the following relative assets' demand function:

$$(A/SA^*)_t = a + b(i_t - i_t^* - \ln E_t S_{t+1} + \ln S_t) + \upsilon_t \qquad (2)$$

where: A = domestic government bonds
A^* = foreign government bonds
υ = disturbance $\rightarrow N(0, \sigma_\upsilon^2)$

Notice that, because of the way (2) is derived, no wealth variable appears in the equation. Therefore, there should be no need to 'proxy wealth' (as done, for instance, in Rogoff (1984)) if one wants to estimate a model based on (2). By the same token, υ need not be autocorrelated owing to the 'omission of wealth' from the equation. Following Frankel (1982), inversion of (2) yields:

$$i_t - i_t^* - \ln E_t S_{t+1} + \ln S_t = \alpha + \beta(A/SA^*)_t + \theta_t \qquad (3)$$

where: $\alpha = -a/b < 0$
$\beta = 1/b > 0$
$\theta = \upsilon/b \rightarrow N(0, \sigma_\upsilon^2/b^2)$

Then, thanks to the (weak-form) hypothesis of rational expectations:

$$\ln S_{t+1} = E_t S_{t+1} + \varepsilon_{t+1} \qquad (4)$$

$$\varepsilon \rightarrow N(0, \sigma_\varepsilon^2), \quad E(\varepsilon_t, \varepsilon_{t+i}) = 0 \quad i = \pm 1$$

Finally, combining (3) with (4):

$$i_t - i_t^* - \ln S_{t+1} + \ln S_t = \alpha + \beta(A/SA^*)_t + \mu_t \qquad (5)$$

where: $\mu_t = \theta_t - \varepsilon_{t+1}$.

Estimating (5) allows us to test the null hypothesis (H_0) of perfect

17

asset substitutability. Under H_0, $b \rightarrow \infty$ (see Appendix 1) and both α and β equal zero. Under H_1: $\alpha < 0$, $\beta > 0$. Rejection of H_0 would thus support the existence of a portfolio-balance link affecting the risk premium. Such a link in turn allows sterilized intervention – which changes the relative supply of assets – to affect the exchange rate. The latter is, in fact, the 'jump' variable which bears the major burden of risk-premium changes.

However, (5) presents some empirical problems. First, (A/SA^*) is correlated with the structural component of the error term via equation (2). Moreover, the right-hand-side variable of the equation will be endogenous as long as S is endogenous. Therefore, an instrumental variable (IV) technique is required to minimize simultaneity bias. (The bias is expected to be negative. In fact, an examination of equations (2) and (5) reveals that plim $[(A/SA^*)_t, \mu_t]$ < 0.) Second, the error term in (5) is likely to be autocorrelated. In fact, there is no way to rule out correlation between the forecast error ε_t revealed at time t and the innovation θ_t, also occurring at t. Therefore, $E(\mu_t, \mu_{t-1}) = \rho_{\theta\varepsilon} \neq 0$, and IV estimation will lack efficiency. Use of standard GLS corrections in the present context would yield inconsistent estimates (see Begg (1982, p. 112)). Cumby, Huizinga and Obstfeld (1983) propose a two-step, two-stage least-squares estimator to cope with both simultaneity and autocorrelation in a rational expectations context. However, I found it computationally easier to proceed as explained below.

I ran regressions of (5) over the ERM sample employing monthly data on France (seen as the domestic country) and Germany. Data sources are reported in Appendix 2. I used end of month observations to avoid overlapping forecast periods. Lack of end of month data on Italian assets prevented me from testing H_0 in the Italy–Germany case too.[12] To proxy A and A^* I used public bonds held by private agents, i.e. outside assets as opposed to all bonds. The point here is that the latter include also (inside) assets which net out within the private sector. Outside assets instead do not net out within the private sector and hence they are homogeneous (from a risk point of view) in the eyes of private investors. In sum, considering outside assets should reduce aggregation problems. It should also be noted that considering public bonds only as opposed to bonds plus monetary base implies the least severe test for accepting H_0 (see Frankel (1982)).

Table 7 Risk-premium equations, France–Germany (1981:3–1987:12)[a]

	Const.	$(A/SA^*)_t$	μ_{t-1}	Dummy	$\bar{R}^2$	SER	DW	BP(12)[b]
OLS	−0.086	0.284			0.219	0.038	1.249	31.52*
	(0.037)	(0.065)						
OLS	−0.063	0.246	0.363		0.308	0.035	1.986	12.9
AR(1)	(0.051)	(0.091)	(0.117)					
IV-1	−0.148	0.393			0.184	0.039	1.217	25.53*
	(0.076)	(0.134)						
IV-2	−0.099	0.284		0.0711	0.637	0.026	1.872	17.09
	(0.05)	(0.088)		(0.008)				

a Autocorrelation correction on OLS AR(1) carried out through the Cochrane–Orcutt procedure. Dependent variable lagged two periods used as instrument for $(A/SA^*)_t$ in IV regressions. Data refer to the last working day in each month. Standard errors in parentheses
b Box–Pierce statistic with twelve degrees of freedom. Critical value at 5% level is 21.03. An asterisk indicates rejection of the null hypothesis of serially independent residuals

Owing to the presence of capital controls in France, one-month Eurointerest rates were used as opposed to domestic ones. Therefore the dependent variable in (5) should capture the risk premium independent of the presence of capital controls. The empirical results are reported in Table 7. The major result is that both $\hat{\alpha}$ and $\hat{\beta}$ almost always turn out to be significantly different from zero and 'correctly' signed – under H_1. This would suggest the presence of a systematic portfolio-balance effect on the FF/DM risk premium.

The OLS estimates in Table 7 are downward biased. Moreover, they are inefficient due – not surprisingly – to autocorrelation problems. The OLS AR(1) estimates cope with autocorrelation only. The DW and BP statistics on OLS AR(1) coupled with the estimate of ρ suggest that the OLS residuals follow an AR(1) process. The IV-1 estimates take care of simultaneity. In fact, both $\hat{\alpha}$ and $\hat{\beta}$ change in magnitude (not in sign) with respect to their OLS estimates while remaining 'significant'. With the IV-2 regression we attempted to cope with both simultaneity and autocorrelation.[13] An examination of the IV-1 residuals revealed that prior to French franc devaluations the fitted values systematically underpredict the actual values. The implied discrete jumps in the risk premium may be due to the thinness of the Eurofranc market

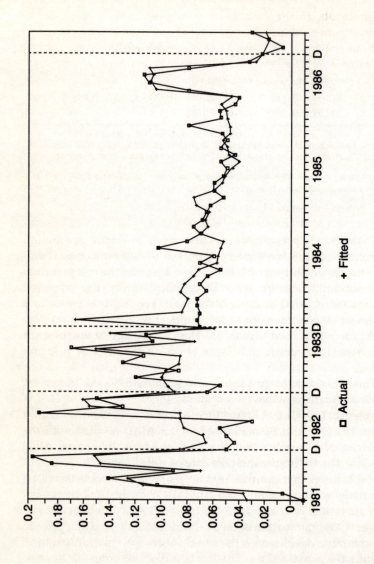

Figure 3 France–Germany regression: actual versus fitted values, March 1983 to August 1986

and consequent variability of the aggregate degree of risk aversion. Therefore, I introduced a dummy variable taking a value of one in the few observations preceding each of the mentioned realignments. The IV-2 estimates show that thanks to the dummy – admittedly not the best way to proxy something which has been 'left out' – I could cope with simultaneity and autocorrelation at the same time. Therefore, the IV-2 estimates should be consistent and more efficient than IV-1. An estimate of β equal to 0.28 implies that – *ceteris paribus* – sterilized intervention which increased $(A/SA^*)_t$ by 10 per cent would, on average, lead to an immediate FF/DM depreciation of 1.6 per cent.[14] Figure 3 shows that the IV-2 fitted values track fairly well the turning points in the risk premium. The figure also shows that the risk premium did jump prior to the franc devaluations (whose dates are indicated by the vertical dashed lines labelled D).

In summary, I would argue that the evidence presented in Table 7 supports the effectiveness of sterilized intervention on the main ERM foreign exchange markets.

So far I have shown that day to day (intramarginal) ERM intervention had been unexpectedly relevant and that the necessary condition for the latter being effective – i.e. a portfolio-balance effect on the risk premium – was plausibly satisfied. This might suffice to restore a 'balance' between the relative importance of capital controls and foreign exchange intervention in stabilizing the ERM.

Although more direct estimates of the extent to which intervention affects exchange rates would be desirable, I am limited by the lack of data on actual intervention.

However, additional indirect evidence may be obtained if one assumes that ERM central banks did intervene, and then tries to detect empirical compatibility between a plausible intervention rule and actual exchange rates' behaviour.

Much of the theoretical literature on intervention assumes that, given a structural model of the economy, the central bank may then intervene in order to minimize a loss function dependent on some ultimate policy goals.

However, such an approach is difficult to implement empirically, especially if one considers different countries simultaneously.[15] Moreover, as long as capital controls are

21

enforced to maintain a degree of policy independence, it seems plausible to think that domestic monetary variables are man-oeuvred to achieve the ultimate goals whilst sterilized intervention is used merely to maintain the ERM parities.

Therefore, I assume that the typical central bank tries to smooth its effective exchange rate by stabilizing two key *bilateral* rates: *vis-à-vis* the DM and *vis-à-vis* the dollar. In particular, I expect an ERM central bank to have given a relatively higher weight to the dollar before 1979 and to the DM thereafter. Although such assumptions may be oversimplifying, consideration of very simple intervention rules is not novel in the literature. For example, Black (1976) argues that a country faced with a combination of real shocks and differential inflation rates should adopt a crawling peg *vis-à-vis* a basket of currencies in order to stabilize the real exchange rate.

Such an intervention rule of thumb would see a central bank trying to affect its effective exchange rate as follows:[16]

$$S_{i,t} = aS(i|\text{DM})_t + (1-a)S(i|\$)_t + \varepsilon_t \qquad (6)$$

where: S_i = effective exchange rate of currency i
$\quad\quad\quad S(i|j)$ = units of i per one unit of j
$\quad\quad\quad 0 \le a \le 1$
$\quad\quad\quad \varepsilon$ = white-noise normally distributed shock

The disturbance should capture those random factors, beyond systematic intervention, which affect the external value of i. Equation (6) can be manipulated to obtain:

$$S_{i,t} = S(i|\$)_t - aS(\text{DM}|\$)_t + \varepsilon_t \qquad (7)$$

Let us now define the steady state for S_i:

$$S_i = \overline{S}_i \qquad (8)$$

In practice, the steady state is never attained owing to the continuous impinging of shocks, news, etc., on the market, but also because (especially ERM) intervention does not necessarily stabilize S_i. Therefore, I assume that between any two periods the steady state is only approached by a factor λ:

$$S_{i,t} - S_{i,t-1} = \lambda(\overline{S}_i - S_{i,t-1}) \qquad (9)$$

with $0 \le \lambda \le 1$ if the process is convergent.

Substituting (7) into (9), after a few manipulations it is possible to obtain:

$$\Delta S(i|\$)_t = \alpha_0 + \alpha_1 \Delta S(DM|\$)_t$$
$$+ \alpha_2 S(i|\$)_{t-1} + \alpha_3 S(DM|\$)_{t-1} - \varepsilon_t + \varphi\varepsilon_{t-1} \qquad (10)$$

where: $\alpha_0 = \lambda S_i \geq 0$
$$0 \leq \alpha_1 = a \leq 1$$
$$\alpha_2 = -\lambda < 0$$
$$\alpha_3 = -\alpha_1\alpha_2 = a\lambda \geq 0$$
$$\varphi = 1 - \lambda$$

Equation (10) is an estimating equation which allows us to estimate $a (= \alpha_1)$, i.e. the parameter is identified. Equation (6) tells us that the parameter a is the weight given to the DM by the intervention rule of thumb. Hence I would expect estimation of (10) for ERM currencies to yield the following results:

1   $0 \leq \alpha_1 \leq 0.5$ before the ERM period;
2   $0.5 \leq \alpha_1 \leq 1$ during the ERM period.

I estimated (10) for the following currencies *vis-à-vis* the dollar: sterling, Swiss franc, French franc, lira and yen. Data are monthly averages over the samples 1974:2–1979:3 and 1979:4–1988:12. All the equations have been estimated by OLS allowing for AR(1) residuals as the derivation of (10) would suggest. SUR estimation did not provide qualitatively different results. The results are presented in Tables 8 and 9.

First of all notice that – having allowed for AR(1) residuals – the obtained estimates are substantially free from autocorrelation. The φ estimate is always 'significant' and positive as the derivation of (10) would suggest. The remaining parameters' estimates are almost always 'correctly' signed, though $\hat{\alpha}_2$ and $\hat{\alpha}_3$ are rarely 'significant' during the pre-ERM period. The equations' explanatory power is satisfactory and increases over the ERM period. The non-linear restriction is rejected only in one case out of ten. All in all, the results are consistent with the view that central banks – particularly after 1979 – may have had effective exchange rate targets to be achieved through interventions carried out in dollars and DMs.

Moreover, the estimates of $\alpha_1 \equiv a$ confirm my expectations. $\hat{\alpha}_1$ is always within its expected range and significantly different from

Table 8 Pre-ERM regressions, 1974:2–1979:3[a]

	α_0	α_1	α_2	α_3	φ	$\bar{R}^2$	SER	DW	W_1[b]
$\Delta S(\$/\pounds)$	-0.013	0.394	-0.036	0.037	0.438	0.41	0.016	1.778	0.259
	(0.042)	(0.1)	(0.073)	(0.027)	(0.123)				
$\Delta S(SF/\$)$	-0.017	0.969	-0.067	0.083	0.553	0.664	0.016	1.865	0.137
	(0.039)	(0.098)	(0.055)	(0.097)	(0.115)				
$\Delta S(FF/\$)$	0.017	0.576	-0.024	0.024	0.34	0.409	0.014	1.981	0.135
	(0.065)	(0.095)	(0.046)	(0.025)	(0.127)				
$\Delta S(L/\$)$	0.01	0.387	-0.005	0.038	0.366	0.287	0.018	1.733	0.84
	(0.192)	(0.113)	(0.026)	(0.033)	(0.125)				
$\Delta S(Y/\$)$	0.344	0.61	-0.078	0.103	0.478	0.361	0.018	1.832	0.259
	(0.29)	(0.12)	(0.064)	(0.089)	(0.124)				

a Standard errors in parentheses
b Wald statistic on the restriction $\alpha_3 = -\alpha_1\alpha_2$. The statistic follows a chi-squared distribution, whose 5% level value is 3.84.

Table 9 Post-ERM inception regressions, 1979:4–1986:12

	α_0	α_1	α_2	α_3	φ	$\bar{R}^2$	SER	DW	$F(1,82)$[a]	W_1
$\Delta S(\$/\pounds)$	0.012	0.633	-0.391	0.147	0.538	0.598	0.018	2.039	13.87*	1.488
	(0.018)	(0.064)	(0.097)	(0.044)	(0.059)					
$\Delta S(SF/\$)$	0.002	1.016	-0.357	0.125	0.567	0.886	0.011	1.953	1.43	3.836
	(0.009)	(0.039)	(0.062)	(0.05)	(0.096)					
$\Delta S(FF/\$)$	0.011	0.982	-0.351	0.024	0.482	0.917	0.009	1.998	151.04*	0.46
	(0.011)	(0.033)	(0.118)	(0.031)	(0.107)					
$\Delta S(L/\$)$	0.217	0.862	-0.371	0.064	0.32	0.918	0.008	2.0	266.5*	6.913*
	(0.081)	(0.029)	(0.14)	(0.023)	(0.106)					
$\Delta S(Y/\$)$	0.155	0.653	-0.291	-0.033	0.536	0.501	0.022	2.066	0.291	0.462
	(0.022)	(0.079)	(0.043)	(0.022)	(0.096)					

a F test for α_1 not being significantly different from its estimated value over the pre-ERM period. An asterisk indicates rejection of the null hypothesis at the 5% level (critical value = 3.95)

zero. The F stability tests and the size of $\hat{\alpha}_1$ in the two sub-periods indicate that until 1979 the DM was never unambiguously the reference currency for foreign exchange market intervention, with the only (unsurprising) exception of Switzerland. However, things do change during the ERM period. The importance of the DM unambiguously grows, overcoming that of the dollar, both for France and Italy and, quite surprisingly, for the UK too.[17] Such results would suggest that the DM gradually assumed the role of major stabilization target. This is quite understandable as far as Italy and France are concerned, implying that imperfect asset substitutability was exploited to intervene in order to influence the FF/DM and L/DM rates. However, the fact that a similar result holds for the UK as well is somewhat surprising. Such a result may imply that – either thanks to sterilized intervention or to explicit monetary policy – sterling tended to behave like an ERM currency. This supports the view that the UK authorities did 'shadow' the ERM for some time before joining the system in 1990.

My main conclusions, however, remain those of (a) evidence that day to day ERM intervention had been more substantial than expected, (b) evidence that the necessary condition for ERM sterilized intervention being effective was satisfied, (c) evidence that (b) may have been exploited by central banks intervening through a simple stabilizing rule of thumb. In my view, such evidence, coupled with the arguments presented in the second section, suggests that the ERM stability of the 1980s did not depend solely on capital controls but also on foreign exchange market intervention. In turn, the latter would have been facilitated by some of the institutional features of the ERM. Of course, it is also possible that national policies had actually been more convergent – as the evidence of the second section would suggest – than sometimes assumed. Were this so, however, the case for capital controls as the only determinant of ERM stability would be further weakened.

CONCLUSIONS

The main scope of this chapter has been to put into a more balanced perspective the relative importance of capital controls, foreign exchange market intervention and monetary convergence as determinants of the ERM stability between 1983 and 1992. The evidence provided in the second section suggests that monetary policies have been more convergent during the ERM period than before. However, 'convergence' does not imply 'cooperation' (see Artis (1986)) and many would argue this is what is needed to gear domestic monetary and fiscal policies towards exchange rate stability. In the second section I also discussed empirical evidence supporting the fairly accepted view that the ERM has indeed secured a previously unexperienced degree of exchange rate stability among member countries. Then, I discussed the commonly held argument that such stability had been secured only thanks to capital controls. I did not deny the role of capital controls, particularly as long as they were actually 'biting'. Prima-facie evidence on this is provided by the divergent behaviour of domestic and Eurointerest rates in the vicinity of an (expected) realignment. (Analogous evidence has already been provided by Giavazzi and Giovannini (1986).)

I have, however, stressed my belief that the importance of capital controls was overstated. First, during the 1970s capital controls (in France and Italy) were no less stringent than in the 1980s, yet exchange rate volatility among Germany, France and Italy was far greater than experienced during the ERM period. Second, the Van Wijnbergen (1985) argument that capital controls are unlikely to stabilize real exchange rates, coupled with evidence of greater real exchange rate stability, implies that such stability must have been achieved through means different from capital controls. I argued that such means may have been foreign exchange market intervention coupled with greater monetary convergence. Such a claim is supported by the fact that some of the ERM institutional features are explicitly geared towards making intervention more effective.

The third section discussed some stylized facts supporting the role of ERM intervention. In particular, I presented empirical evidence consistent with the presence, on the major ERM currency markets, of a risk premium whose main determinant is the relative supply of outside assets. This portfolio-balance channel (independent of the presence of controls on capital flows) satisfies the necessary condition for sterilized intervention to be effective. I also presented empirical evidence showing that actual exchange

27

rates' behaviour has been consistent with the assumption that central banks intervened following a simple rule of thumb. In particular the results support the view that, after 1979, the behaviour of ERM central banks started to reflect the new exchange rate constraints.

My major conclusion is, therefore, that capital controls cannot alone have secured exchange rate stability within the ERM. It is likely that intervention played a role in that sense, though one often neglected. Were this so, it would be possible to argue that a complete removal of capital controls (from countries like Ireland, Portugal and Spain) should not, by itself, jeopardize the ERM, very much like after the removal of Italian and French controls at the turn of the 1980s.

APPENDIX 1

Equation (2) in the text can be derived as follows. Consider a two-country portfolio-balance model aggregating across domestic and foreign agents with four assets traded. If agents are wealth (mean–variance) optimizers, bond demands are functions of the risk premium only (see Frankel (1983)). All the parameters are positive.

$$(M/W)_t = f(.) \tag{A.1}$$

$$(A/W)_t = \beta_0 + \beta_1 [(1 + i_t)/(1 + i_t^*) - E_t S_{t+1}/S_t] \tag{A.2}$$

$$(SA^*/W)_t = \gamma_0 - \gamma_1 [(1 + i_t)/(1 + i_t^*) - E_t S_{t+1}/S_t] \tag{A.3}$$

$$(SM^*/W)_t = g(.) \tag{A.4}$$

$$W_t = M_t + A_t + SA_t^* + SM_t^* \tag{A.5}$$

where: M = domestic money supply
A = domestic bonds supply
SA^* = foreign bonds supply, in domestic currency
SM^* = foreign money supply, in domestic currency
W = financial wealth

Note that in the case of perfect substitutability between A and A^*: $\beta_1 = \gamma_1 \to \infty$.

Thanks to Walras's law I can drop (A.4). Then let us subtract (A.3) from (A.2):

$$(A/W)_t - (SA^*/W)_t = \varphi_0 + \varphi_1 [(1 + i_t)/(1 + i_t^*) - E_t S_{t+1}/S_t] \qquad (A.6)$$

where: $\varphi_1 = \beta_1 + \gamma_1 (\rightarrow \infty$ in the case of perfect substitutability)
$\quad\quad\quad \varphi_0 = \beta_0 - \gamma_0 > 0^{18}$

Now I can solve (A.1) for M and substitute for the latter into (A.5). Then, I substitute for the resulting W_t expression into (A.6) and take logarithms, thus obtaining:

$$\ln(A/SA^*)_t = \ln \varphi_0 + \varphi_1(RP) \qquad (A.7)$$

$$RP = i_t - i_t^* - \ln E_t S_{t+1} + \ln S_t \qquad (A.8)$$

Taking anti-logarithms (A.7) becomes:

$$(A/SA^*)_t = \exp[\ln \varphi_0 + \varphi_1(RP)] \qquad (A.9)$$

We can now linearize (A.9) taking its first-order expansion around $RP = 0$:

$$
\begin{aligned}
(A/SA^*)_t &= \exp(\ln \varphi_0) + \varphi_1[\exp(\ln \varphi_0)](RP - 0) \\
&= \exp(\ln \varphi_0) + \varphi_1[\exp(\ln \varphi_0)]RP
\end{aligned} \qquad (A.10)
$$

Recalling (A.8), (A.10) can be rewritten as:

$$(A/SA^*)_t = a + b(i_t - i_t^* - \ln E_t S_{t+1} + \ln S_t) \qquad (A.11)$$

where: $a = \exp(\ln \varphi_0) > 0,$ for $\beta_0 > \gamma_0$
$\quad\quad\quad b = \varphi_1[\exp(\ln \varphi_0)] \rightarrow \infty,$ if A and A^* are perfect substitutes

(A.11) is equation (2) reported in the text apart from the error term.

APPENDIX 2

Data sources

All exchange rates: End of month and monthly averages from *International Financial Statistics*.

Eurointerest rates: End of month (monthly averages for Figures 1 and 2), one-month maturity, from *Analystics* data base, Chase Econometrics.

German outside assets: Public bonds in circulation (minus public holdings), end of month, from *Monthly Report of the Deutsche Bundesbank*.

French outside assets: Public bonds in circulation (minus public holdings), end of month, from INSEE, *Bulletin Mensuel de Statistique.*

2

THE EFFECTIVENESS OF CAPITAL CONTROLS
An empirical analysis of the ERM

INTRODUCTION

Over the last few years, a series of studies have addressed questions on controls on international capital flows. Choice-theoretic models have been used to analyse the welfare implications of controls, the way they affect the international transmission of fiscal policies, and their impact on devaluation policies. The second section of this chapter will recall some of the issues which are more thoroughly surveyed in Dornbusch (1986) and Edwards (1989).

Regrettably, the growing body of theory has scarcely been paralleled by empirical studies, thus undermining the reliability of policy prescriptions. In particular, doubts on the effectiveness of capital and foreign exchange controls have had a bearing on debates over the Exchange Rate Mechanism (ERM) of the European Monetary System (EMS). Yet, conclusions on this point have often been drawn without the aid of empirical knowledge.

The only evidence available has been that of deviations from parity conditions on foreign exchange markets – notably in France and Italy – thus capturing only the *price* and not the *quantity* effect of controls. Nevertheless, it has been commonplace to claim that the main factor of stability of the ERM has been the safety net provided by capital and foreign exchange controls.

This received wisdom hardly squares with results from earlier research. First, Gros (1987, 1988) provided a theoretical framework in which capital and foreign exchange controls lose their effectiveness in the long run. Second, the previous chapter has presented evidence indicating that the received wisdom overstates the

31

effectiveness of controls as a factor of ERM stability. Finally, developments following the scrapping of controls in France and Italy suggest that foreign exchange liberalization *per se* hardly destabilized the ERM.

This chapter presents further evidence suggesting that the long-run effectiveness of controls vanished as early as in 1985. This carries obvious implications for managing the ERM and, more generally, for the long-run usefulness of those tools of policy. Such implications are stressed in the fifth section of this chapter whilst the next section brings together issues relevant to this study. The third section presents the capital controls model whose estimation results are discussed in the fourth section.

REVIEW OF THE ISSUES

It is useful to start by drawing a distinction between capital controls and foreign exchange controls.[1] Although the literature often uses the two terms indifferently, the underlying concepts are quite different. Capital controls affect capital flows via differential tax treatments involving withholding taxes, reserve ratios, or the use of different exchange rates for current and capital account transactions (dual exchange rates).[2] On the other hand, foreign exchange controls 'physically' limit the amount of (foreign) assets which agents can acquire. If biting, these controls create a wedge between offshore and onshore interest rates. In contrast to this, the yield differential generated by capital controls is generally less significant albeit relatively more stable.

An example of the gap in yields created by differential tax treatments is that typically prevailing between Eurodeutschmark and (German) domestic interest rates as a result of reserve requirements imposed by the Bundesbank on banks located in Germany. That difference is usually no higher than fifty basis points. Against this, the wedge between offshore and onshore short-term interest rates caused by the foreign exchange controls enforced in France and Italy exceeded, on occasions, twenty percentage points.

In the light of such evidence one should generally expect foreign exchange controls to be more binding than capital controls. Further support for this view comes from theoretical work by

By substituting for (14) into (11) the problem becomes one of maximizing:

$$\sum_{t}^{\infty}\{B_{t-1}(1+i_{t-1})(1+i_t) + B_{t-1}^*[(1+i_{t-1}^*)S_t](1+i_t)$$

$$+ \Delta B_t(1+i_t) + S_t\Delta B_t^*(1+i_t) - (\phi/2)S_t\Delta B_t^{*2}(1+i_t)$$

$$- (\phi/2)S_t\Delta B_t^{*2} + B_t^*[(1+i_t^*)S_{t+1}^e - (1+i_t)S_t]\}A^t \tag{15}$$

The choice variables are B and B^*. Thanks to A being the discount rate which equates returns at consecutive dates we can obtain the Euler equation determining capital outflows (ΔB^*):

By using the lag operator ($L^iX_t \equiv X_{t-i}, L^{-i}X_t \equiv X_{t+i}$), the difference equation (16) can be transformed as follows:

$$(S\Delta B^*)_t = [-1/(\phi A)][1/(L^{-1} - 1/A)][(1+i_t^*)S_{t+1}^e$$

$$- (1+i_t)S_t] - Z(1/A)^t \tag{17}$$

where Z is an arbitrary constant the value of which can be imposed at zero in order to induce boundedness in $(S\Delta B^*)$ as long as the expression enclosed in the last square brackets is a bounded sequence. By further algebraical manipulation and exploiting the fact that $1/(1 - AL^{-1}) = 1 + AL + A^2L^{-2} + A^3L^{-3} + \dots$ it is possible to arrive at:

$$(S\Delta B^*)_t = (1/\phi) \sum_{t}^{\infty} A^t[(1+i_t^*)S_{t+1}^e - (1+i_t)S_t] \tag{18}$$

Since it can be empirically shown that the expression in the last square brackets follows an AR(1) process – with ε as the autoregressive parameter – the solution can be expressed in the following observable form (noting that $0 < A \equiv 1/(1+r) < 1$):

$$(S\Delta B^*)_t = \{1/[\phi(1-\varepsilon A)]\}[(1+i_t^*)S_{t+1}^e - (1+i_t)S_t] \tag{19}$$

The foreign investor faces a maximization problem analogous to that of the domestic investor:

$$\text{Max } W^* = \sum_{t=0}^{\infty} \{B_t^*(1+i_t^*) + (B_t/S_t)(1+i_t)(1/S_{t+1}^e)/(1/S_t)]$$

$$+ (\Omega/2)\Delta(B/S)_t^2\}A^t$$

$$= \sum_{t=0}^{\infty} \{B_t^*(1 + i_t^*) + [B_t(1 + i_t)/S_{t+1}^e] - (\Omega/2)\Delta(B/S)_t^2\}A^t \qquad (20)$$

Note that the parameter capturing the cost of controls (Ω) differs from that relevant to the domestic agent (ϕ), thus implying that controls impinge asymmetrically on outflows and inflows. (This presumption is justified by a cursory examination of foreign exchange laws in France and Italy.) The estimates presented in the next section will provide a more formal check of this asymmetry hypothesis. Maximization of (20) is subject to constraints similar to those imposed on (11):

$$W_t^* = B_t/S_t + B_t^* \qquad (21)$$

$$W_t^* = W_{t-1}^* R_{t-1}^* + \Delta(B/S)_t + \Delta B_t^* - (\Omega/2)\Delta(B/S)_t^2 \qquad (22)$$

By focusing on the choice variable B it is possible to obtain the Euler equation explaining the acquisition of domestic assets:[9]

$$\Delta B_t = (1/\Omega) \sum_{t}^{\infty} A_t[(1 + i_t)/S_{t+1}^e(1 + i_t^*)/S_t]$$

$$= \{1/[\Omega(1 - \tau A)]\}[(1 + i_t)/S_{t+1}^e - (1 + i_t^*)/S_t] \qquad (23)$$

In order to aggregate across agents it is useful to impose economy-wide constraints. Since equations (19) and (23) explain much of the capital account, it helps to start by writing down the balance of payments identity before introducing further behaviour into the model.

$$CA_t + KA_t = \Delta FX_t \qquad (24)$$

where CA = current account, KA = capital account, FX = official reserves. In conformity with standard open-economy macroeconomics, the current account is assumed to be determined by relative incomes and the real effective exchange rate:

$$CA_t = \mu + \alpha(SY^*/Y)_t \pm \beta(P/SP^*)_t \qquad (25)$$

where Y = domestic GDP, y^* = foreign GDP, P = domestic wholesale price index, P^* = foreign wholesale price index, and μ is a constant to proxy net 'invisibles'. The ambiguity in the sign on the real exchange rate coefficient reflects uncertainty over the Marshall–Lerner condition. The capital account is largely determined by the flows underlying equations (19) and (23):

$$KA_t = \theta + \Delta B_t - (S\Delta B^*)_t - \delta\Delta SE_t \qquad (26)$$

where θ is a constant to proxy net errors and omissions and direct investment whilst $\delta\Delta SE_t$ (SE being the nominal effective exchange rate) aims at capturing valuation changes in official reserves, normally appearing under 'counterpart items'.[10]

Finally, combining equations (19) and (23) with the balance of payments bloc of equations (24) to (26) leads to the following estimating equation:

$$\Delta FX_t = (\theta + \mu) + \alpha(SY^*/Y)_t \pm \beta(P/SP^*)_t - \sigma_1[(1 + i_t^*)S_{t+1}^e$$

$$- (1 + i_t)S_t] + \sigma_2[(1 + i_t)/S_{t+1}^e - (1 + i_t^*)/S_t] - \delta\Delta SE_t \qquad (27)$$

where $\sigma_1 = 1/[\phi(1 - \varepsilon A)] > 0$, and $\sigma_2 = 1/[\Omega(1 - \tau A)] > 0$.

Note that when both ϕ and Ω tend to zero, i.e. controls are completely ineffective, both σ_1 and σ_2 tend to infinity; B and B^* become thus perfectly substitutable in international portfolios. The opposite holds when both ϕ and Ω tend to infinity, i.e. when controls are infinitely effective B and B^* become completely unsubstitutable. Here there is a parallel with asset demand functions derived from mean–variance optimization where the demand for a given asset depends on the expected return (the risk premium) whose coefficient measures the degree of asset substitutability. Indeed, the variables attached to both σ_1 and σ_2 are linear transformations of the risk premium. Hence the σ_is capture the degree of asset substitutability which in this particular model is affected by the stringency of controls.

Note also that:

$$\delta\sigma_1/\delta\phi = -1/[\phi^2(1 - \varepsilon A)] < 0, \quad \delta\sigma_2/\delta\Omega = -1/[\Omega^2(1 - \tau A)] < 0 \qquad (28)$$

Therefore, a tightening of controls on domestic agents, i.e. an increase in ϕ, will boost official reserves *ceteris paribus* only if the term attached to σ_1 is positive, which requires $(1 + i_t)$ to be smaller than $(1 + i^*)S_{t+1}^e/S_t$. In other words, a tightening of domestic controls serves its purpose only if domestic interest rates are 'low'.[11] This formalizes the received wisdom that controls increase the degree of monetary policy independence. Such independence can be used to boost growth in the domestic economy whilst relaxing the balance of payments constraint. According to this model, however, tightening controls would be ill-judged if accompanied by unnecessarily high domestic interest rates.

Another implication of equation (27) is that, if $\text{cov}(\phi, \Omega) > 0$, the boost to official reserves from tightening domestic controls when $(1 + i_t) < (1 + i_t^*)(S_{t+1}^e / S_t)$ is reinforced by the expression attached to σ_2 being negative. Vice versa, were domestic interest rates 'too high', a simultaneous increase in ϕ and Ω would have a mutually reinforcing detrimental effect on official reserves.

To sum up, fine tuning domestic controls can improve the overall balance of payments only if domestic interest rates are kept 'low'. Moreover, the effect of such policies is strengthened if the costs of controls perceived by domestic agents (ϕ) is positively correlated with that of foreign agents (Ω).

Estimating equation (27) enables us to verify the empirical effectiveness of controls in two ways. First, by assessing the significance of ϕ and Ω and their evolution through time. Second, by comparing the path of official reserves from simulating (27) against the path generated by the same equation with the σ_is constrained to values as if there were no controls at all, i.e. as if domestic and foreign assets were perfect substitutes. The gap between the two simulated paths can then be attributed to the impact of controls on capital flows.

EMPIRICAL RESULTS

Equation (27) was estimated on French and Italian quarterly data whose details are provided in the appendix to this chapter. The sample periods were 1977:1–1989:4 and 1974:1–1989:4 respectively, the French data being shorter owing to the unavailability of earlier data on the real effective exchange rate of the franc. The equation was estimated by a maximum likelihood (ML) estimator.[12] Data on expected future exchange rates are one-step-ahead forecasts from ARIMA models thereby assuming weakly rational expectations. Moreover, instrumental variables were used for domestic interest rates so as to dampen the bias due to short-term interest rates possibly being the dependent variable of a policy reaction function targeting the level of official reserves. Instruments were lagged domestic interest rates, foreign interest rates, the nominal effective exchange rate and official reserves. Finally, the rate of discount (r) was assumed to equal the sample average between domestic and foreign interest rates.

The foreign counterpart to both France and Italy was taken as being the OECD area as far as GDP is concerned and the set of relevant trade partners as far as effective exchange rates are concerned. However, composite measures are not available for the 'risk-premium' terms attached to the σ_i. In this case, we considered the foreign sector as comprising the USA, Germany and the UK – the countries most likely to have substantial capital flows with France and Italy.[13] Then, a general-to-specific approach was applied to equation (27) starting with six (excluding lags) risk-premium terms to end up only with those significantly different from zero.

Let us consider the French case first. Following Claassen and Wyplosz (1982), controls in France can be split between those impinging on banks and those affecting non-banks. The corner-stone of the former was the proscription of an overall open position in foreign currency. To toughen controls, the Banque de France would occasionally check the positions banks can take *vis-à-vis* individual non-residents. As foreigners could speculate by borrowing francs or, equivalently, selling them forward, preventing domestic banks from entering such contracts would reduce the 'speculative' supply of francs to non-residents. Controls on non-banks focused on constraining tourism-related transactions, transfers, holding of foreign assets, forward cover, and leads and lags in trade-related foreign currency transactions.

French controls had been in place on and off since 1939 with the latest uninterrupted spell lasting from 1968 to the end of 1989. In the early 1970s, controls aimed at reducing upward pressure on the franc as the dollar was under attack. From August 1971 to March 1974 a two-tier exchange rate regime was in place. Thereafter, controls remained virtually unchanged until 1981 and were geared towards limiting capital outflows.

In 1981, following the election of President Mitterand, controls were tightened to their strongest degree. In May, the *divise-titre* regime – whereby only proceeds from the sale of foreign assets could be used to finance new purchases – was introduced alongside the requirement that 75 per cent of direct investment abroad had to be financed through foreign currency borrowing. In September, abolition of the forward cover of imports could not prevent a devaluation of the franc the following month. Controls were further tightened in March 1982 with the time limit for the surrender of foreign currency by exporters reduced to only two weeks, 100 per cent of direct investment abroad to be financed via foreign currency loans, and capital outflows for the purchase of real estate made subject to state authorization.

A final slight tightening followed the devaluation of the franc in March 1983 but some relaxation started in December with increases in tourism allowances and the abolition of the foreign exchange record system. More decisive steps towards liberalization[14] were taken in 1984 whilst a major liberalization package under an initiative of the Chirac government was introduced in 1986. In particular, domestic agents' purchases of foreign real estate were freed together with the ability to make gifts to non-residents; forward cover of both commercial and financial transactions was completely freed, and the time limits for surrendering foreign currency earnings were extended to three months. During 1987, constraints on foreign direct investment and the *divise-titre* regime on portfolio investment were removed whilst 1988 saw French companies gaining full freedom to deal in foreign currency and banks being allowed to make loans to non-residents. The remaining controls were scrapped at the end of 1989, thus allowing domestic households to open bank accounts abroad and foreign currency accounts at home. Liberalization was, therefore, completed ahead of the EC deadline of July 1990.

Table 10 presents the model's estimates on France. Equation (27) was augmented by adding a dummy variable to the list of regressors. Note that in no way does the dummy capture the stringency of controls. In fact, it takes the value of one in 1982:4, when the fitted values significantly underpredicted capital inflows, reflecting a one-off 6 billion dollar international loan to France. Looking at regression (A), the signs of the estimated parameters conform with theoretical priors although the absolute size of δ looks too high. The negative long-run value for β indicates that a real depreciation ultimately improves the French balance of payments.

Both parameters capturing the costs of controls are positive and significant with ϕ bigger than Ω. This suggests that French controls were indeed effective over the sample period and that the costs on

Table 10 ML estimates of the capital control model*

| | France | | Italy | |
	(A)	(B)	(A)	(B)
α_0	3.15	3.31		
	(2.1)	(2.1)		
α_1			2.76	3.20
			(4.8)	(5.2)
β_0			3.16	3.40
			(9.4)	(9.6)
β_2	−1.86	−1.77		
	(−3.5)	(−3.0)		
β_4	0.70	0.77		
	(1.4)	(1.4)		
ϕ	2.74		143.3	
	(2.3)		(3.5)	
π		2.70		120.2
		(2.3)		(3.3)
Ω	0.06	0.06	0.001	0.01
	(4.3)	(3.2)	(3.4)	(3.1)
δ_0			−2.4	−2.70
			(−7.7)	(−8.2)
δ_3	−5.65	−5.55	−1.52	−1.80
	(−3.8)	(−3.5)	(−3.4)	(−3.9)
δ_4			3.70	4.41
			(7.7)	(9.1)
τ	0.27	0.25		
	(2.5)	(2.1)		
t		0.93		0.90
		(2.9)		(1.9)
t^2		−0.02		−0.02
		(−2.0)		(−1.8)
t^3				−0.0002
				(−1.9)

* Intercept and dummy coefficients not reported. τ is the coefficient on the lagged dependent variable. Subscripts indicate the lag order; superscripts indicate the power order of time trends. T statistics are in parentheses.

domestic agents were higher than those borne by non-residents. Interestingly enough, estimating the model on the post-1983 period yielded parameter estimates of comparable size with the exception of ϕ and Ω which fell to 1.5 and 0.03 respectively (ϕ resulting insignificantly different from zero). It would appear that the effectiveness of controls abated from 1983 onwards.

Regression (B) checks whether that was indeed the case by allowing the estimated value of ϕ to vary through time. This is achieved by expressing the coefficient σ_1 as $1/\{(1 - A)[\pi + f(t)]\}$ where $\phi \equiv \pi + f(t)$, $f(t)$ being a polynomial of the ith order in the time trend.[15] Allowing ϕ to vary improved the fit of the equation whilst leaving the other parameter estimates almost unchanged. The (B) estimates allow the cost of controls to be expressed as a function of time ($\pi + 0.93t - 0.02t^2$). Such new measurement of ϕ is plotted against time in Figure 4 which shows that the stringency of controls rose at the turn of the 1970s, reached its maximum between 1982 and 1983 and declined steeply thereafter. Indeed, by the end of the sample period controls on domestic agents were completely ineffective with ϕ nearing zero. Not only does such a picture fit what one might expect given the actual history of controls in France, it also squares with Cody's (1989) estimates of political risk peaking in 1981–2.

An alternative way to appreciate the evolving role of French controls is provided in Figure 5. This plots the profile of official reserves as simulated by equation (27) – the 'actual' case – against the profile simulated by (27) were the σ_is assigned values which would prevail in the case of highly substitutable assets[16] – the 'no-controls' case. The result of this exercise supports the view that controls did matter during the early 1980s when the profile of official reserves would have been much lower had controls not been in place. However, the opposite held in the post-1986 period. Preserving controls while their effectiveness on domestic agents was fading simply deterred foreigners from buying franc assets, thus preventing capital inflows which the ruling returns would have otherwise secured.

In conclusion, my results indicate that French controls had been almost ineffective in checking capital outflows since 1986 and that the franc exchange rate and/or France's external balance would have been stronger without controls.

Let us now turn to the Italian case. Compared with France, controls in Italy were more complex and finely tuned. Micossi and Rossi (1987) suggest that the original policy objective was to contain savings within the domestic boundaries, hence achieving an 'acceptable' capital account balance. The latter was deemed

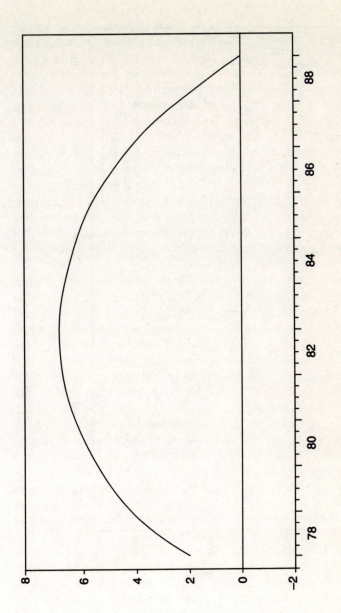

Figure 4 France, capital controls parameter φ

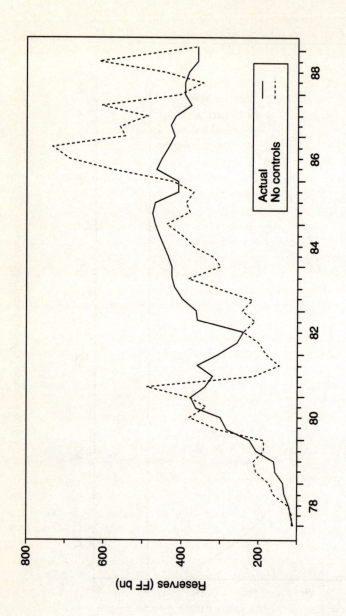

Figure 5 France, actual versus no-controls case

necessary in order to finance the current account deficits induced by expansionary domestic policies. In later years, the main objective became that of containing the volatility of domestic interest rates so as to ease the financing of huge public deficits.

The Italian system of controls, in force since the 1930s, was substantially dismantled in the early 1960s. However, the process of liberalization took a U-turn at the end of that decade owing to a deterioration in the external balance. In 1972, lira banknotes were declared inconvertible in an attempt to stop their illegal export. The year of 1973 saw the introduction of a dual exchange market (removed the following year), the reduction of leads and lags in export and import payments, the requirement that bank foreign assets and liabilities be balanced daily, and a compulsory non-interest-rate-bearing deposit with the Banca d'Italia amounting to 50 per cent of every investment abroad. Barring a short respite in 1975, the situation deteriorated further over the next three years. Compulsory non-interest-bearing deposits often had to be extended to imports of goods whilst the net foreign currency debtor position of banks was often frozen. Such measures were supplemented with tighter ceilings on foreign exchange allowances for tourism, compulsory foreign exchange financing of exports, and taxes on foreign exchange purchases. The lira crisis culminated with the closure of the foreign exchange market between January and March 1976.

Some controls could be relaxed between 1977 and 1979 thanks to an improved current account. However, a new tightening took place between 1980 and 1982 with much of the old armoury reactivated. The period from 1983 can be seen as one of foreign exchange liberalization barring two short-lived setbacks in 1985 and 1986. May 1987 marked a turning point as wide-ranging liberalizing steps were taken with regard to compulsory deposits, export financing and tourism allowances. The penultimate controls were lifted in January 1990 by allowing residents to purchase short-term bonds denominated in foreign currency. The ban on opening bank deposits in foreign currency and/or out of Italy was scrapped in July 1990.

The right half of Table 10 presents the estimates of equation (27) on Italy. As in France's case a dummy variable was used. However, as for France, in no way does the dummy capture the stringency of controls; rather the opposite. In fact, the dummy takes the value of one in 1986:1, a period of sudden pressure against the lira when official reserves dropped by 9.5 trillion lire.

The signs of the estimated coefficients agree with theoretical priors. In particular, the values of ϕ and Ω are both positive and significant with the cost of controls on capital outflows being much greater than that on inflows. Again, estimating (27) on a sub-sample starting in 1983 yielded much lower estimates for both ϕ (24.8) and Ω (0.0002), thus suggesting that the effectiveness of controls declined over time.

This is confirmed by the estimates reported in column (B) which refer to a version of (27) where ϕ is allowed to vary with time as done for France. The resulting plot of ϕ (see Figure 6) confirms that the stringency of Italian controls peaked in 1978–9, to abate thereafter. This is roughly what one would expect given the history of foreign exchange regulations sketched above. Major puzzles concerning the results on Italy are the high absolute size of the parameter ϕ and the fact that, albeit falling, the latter still appears to be greater than zero near the sample end. ϕ being still significantly positive in 1989 might reflect the low credibility attached to domestic policies owing to the endemic weakness of Italy's coalition governments.

Figure 7 compares the actual path of official reserves with that which would have prevailed had controls been absent. As for France, the simulation for the no-controls case was carried out by imposing values to the 'risk-premium' terms in (27) consistent with those typical of US and German outside assets. Quite strikingly, it would appear that, far from boosting reserves, controls constrained them on a lower path than would have been the case under a liberal regime – given the historical constellation of exchange and interest rates. However, the paradox may be only apparent. Remember that the derivative (28) shows how a tightening of controls on domestic agents will 'work' only if domestic interest rates are 'low', i.e. if there is a negative risk premium. As Figure 8 shows, this was hardly the case for the lira between 1981 and 1985. Therefore, it should be no surprise that tightening controls in those years did more harm than good. Tighter controls were redundant given the high domestic interest rates; rather than checking capital outflows those measures scared foreign capital

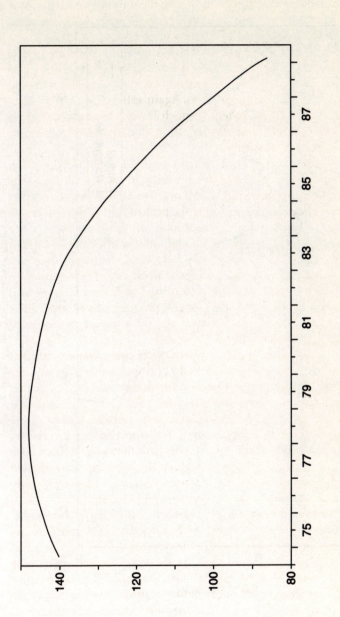

Figure 6 Italy, capital controls parameter φ

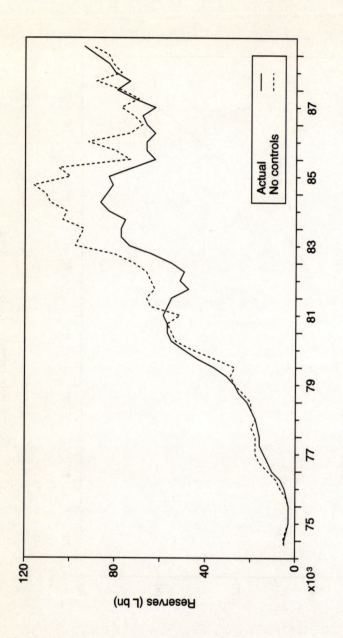

Figure 7 Italy, actual versus no-controls case

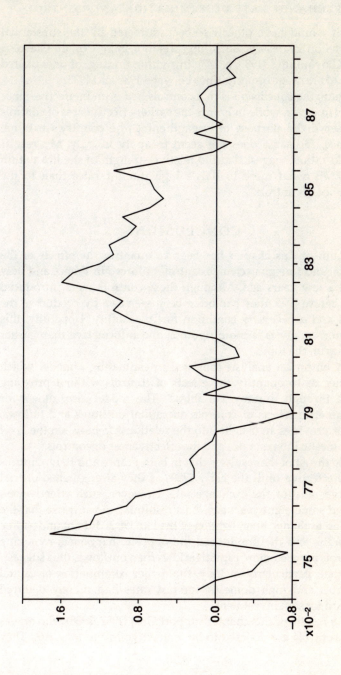

Figure 8 Lira/DM, *ex post risk premium*

which would have otherwise been attracted by the substantial returns on lira assets. Such interpretation may explain Giavazzi and Giovannini's (1989, p. 177) 'intriguing finding' of unexploited inward arbitrage opportunities between 1983 and 1985.

Again, the conclusion is that controls had been ineffective since 1986. However, while in France the earlier effectiveness of controls did serve the purpose of strengthening the country's external balance, the same does not seem to apply to Italy. My results would rather suggest that the relative strength of the lira within the EMS owed more to Italy's high interest rates than to the presence of controls.[17]

CONCLUSIONS

The aim of this chapter has been to quantify the effects of the capital and foreign exchange controls enforced in France and Italy until a few years ago. Although those controls were introduced well before 1979, they had often been seen as a by-product of the ERM and a necessary condition for its stability. Hopefully, this chapter's analysis is more rigorous and informative than earlier studies on the topic.

My empirical analysis consisted in estimating a model which enables us to quantify the effects of controls without proxying them through dummy variables.[18] The model also allows for asymmetric effects of controls on capital outflows and inflows, and it provides an insight into the relationship between the level of domestic interest rates and the effectiveness of controls.

The thrust of the results is that in both France and Italy, controls were effective until the early 1980s as they strengthened official reserves and/or the exchange rate. However, such effectiveness abated some eight years ago. As a result, it is no surprise that the foreign exchange liberalization of the late 1980s did not undermine the franc and the lira. Indeed the opposite happened; removing controls aroused more capital inflows than outflows, thus suggesting that, particularly in Italy, the earlier combination of capital controls and high domestic interest rates had merely deterred inward foreign investment.

The results of this chapter support Gros (1987, 1988) who argues that controls are doomed to be ineffective in the long run. They also support results from Chapter 1 and Giavazzi and Spaventa (1990) which suggest, from different angles, that the complete removal of foreign exchange and capital controls would not *by itself* threaten the ERM. However, our results do not mean that controls are of no use as short-term, anti-speculative devices. As suggested by the EC Commission (1988), the short-run effectiveness of controls is key in allowing ERM monetary authorities to gain time during periods of acute exchange rate pressure. At such times, capital controls slow down the pace of reserves' depletion, thus facilitating 'timely realignments'. These cause only small changes to the central rate (relative to the fluctuation band) such that the market exchange rate does not undergo a discrete change. As a result, the short-term insulating properties of controls can help central bankers to avoid offering one-way bets to foreign exchange speculators.

APPENDIX 3

Data sources

France

P/SP* = franc real effective exchange rate, IFS series via Datastream (FRI65UM.F).

SE = franc nominal effective exchange rate, IFS series via Datastream (FRI..AHX).

S = franc bilateral exchange rates, IFS line rf.

FX = official reserves, Datastream (FRRESERV).

Y = domestic real GDP, Datastream (FRAGDPRODD).

Y* = OECD real GDP, 1985 prices and exchange rates, Main Economic Indicators via Datastream.

i = domestic interbank interest rate, IFS series, line 60b, via Datastream (FRI60BS).

i* = foreign (USA, UK and Germany) three-month interest rate; respectively from IFS, *Financial Statistics* (table 13.8, ajnd), and *Monthly Report of the Deutsche Bundesbank* (table V.6).

Italy

P/SP^* = lira real effective exchange rate, Banca d'Italia, *Bollettino Economico* (table A.16).

SE = lira nominal effective exchange rate, Banca d'Italia, *Bollettino Economico* (table A.19).

S = lira bilateral exchange rates, IFS line rf.

FX = official reserves, Banca d'Italia, *Bollettino Economico* (table A.18), via Datastream.

Y = domestic real GDP, *Main Economic Indicators*.

Y^* = OECD real GDP, 1985 prices and exchange rates, *Main Economic Indicators*, via Datastream.

i = domestic interbank interest rate, IFS, line 60b.

i^* = foreign (USA, UK and Germany) three-month interest rate; respectively from IFS, *Financial Statistics* (table 13.8, ajnd), and *Monthly Report of the Deutsche Bundesbank* (table V.6).

3

EXCHANGE RATE DETERMINATION
Monetary or portfolio-balance effects?

INTRODUCTION

Following the collapse of the Bretton Woods system, the growing importance of capital flows unrelated to real trade transactions favoured the development of asset market theories of exchange rate determination. Among those, the monetary approach sees exchange rate movements as balancing demand and supply for domestic and foreign monetary assets. Instead, the portfolio-balance approach posits that domestic and foreign monies are not the only imperfectly substitutable assets in multi-currency portfolios. If also domestic and foreign bonds are imperfect substitutes then portfolio disequilibria will spark exchange rate changes. All said, in both approaches the exchange rate moves so as to make existing assets willingly held in international portfolios.

It is not my intention to review the empirical research on exchange rate determination models.[1] It will suffice here to recall that monetary models had some degree of success in the 1970s (see e.g. Frankel (1979)) while the 1980s saw empirical support for those models crumble.[2] Isard (1986) concluded that empirical models explain little of the observed variability in exchange rates and that they struggle to match the forecast performance of simple random-walk rules. Empirical portfolio-balance models proved even less successful than monetary ones, both through exchange-rate-reduced forms (see Branson, Halttunen and Masson (1977, 1979)) as well as inverted bond demand, or risk-premium, equations (see Rogoff (1984)). Attempts at synthesizing the monetary and portfolio-balance approaches led to mixed results – see Hooper and Morton (1982) and Frankel (1983, 1984).

Later research did not produce more encouraging results. Particularly disappointing is the inability to formulate a unified theory of exchange rate determination. In other words, whenever researchers 'accept' an empirical model this does not fit more than one exchange rate. MacDonald and Taylor (1992) conclude their review stating that

> asset-approach models have performed well for some time periods, such as the interwar period, and, to some extent, for the … 1973–78 [period]; but they have proved largely inadequate explanations for the behaviour of the major exchange rates for the latter part of the float.

As a possible explanation for recent failures they quote evidence that foreign exchange market investors rely on fundamental analysis (i.e. economic models as opposed to chartism/time series models) mainly for longer-term forecasts. As a result, it could be more fruitful to model the long-run determinants of exchange rates, perhaps using lower-frequency data.

This chapter does just that. I use quarterly data on the DM/dollar and yen/dollar exchange rates and cointegration techniques (pioneered in Engle and Granger (1987)) to model the long-run, equilibrium, determinants of exchange rates. The analysis below builds upon Radaelli (1988) which took issue with two main conclusions from the empirical research of the 1980s. First, that no exchange rate theory is fully supported by the data and, second, that no structural model can outperform a random-walk rule in forecasting. That paper showed how previous studies were flawed by imposing, without prior testing, various types of restriction. The study emphasized the importance of both misspecification and specification tests in model building while bringing the concept of cointegration into the picture. Asset market models, mostly in the monetary mould, were tested, along with VARs, on monthly data between 1973 and 1987 for the DM/dollar and yen/dollar rates. That research confirmed the first of the two aforementioned conclusions: no theory was supported by the data. However, some of the models obtained significantly outperformed the random-walk rule in forecasting.

This chapter departs from Radaelli (1988) in four ways. First, it tests more thoroughly for the variables' order of integration and

uncovered interest parity is replaced by a demand equation for (net) foreign assets plus the assumption that the latter's supply equals the balance of payments, in turn determined by relative incomes and the real exchange rate. It is thanks to the latter that, in Driskill's model, an increase (decrease) in p leads to a depreciation (appreciation) of s. We refer to (35) as the Dornbusch–Driskill model which can accommodate both sign constellations on p and p^*.

Thus far, portfolio-balance elements have appeared only superficially in the Hooper–Morton and Driskill models. Let us now introduce a fully fledged portfolio-balance model.[7] This model builds upon the non-perfect substitutability of outside (financial) assets, i.e. public debt. As a result, there will be extra variables, in addition to those of the monetary model, affecting the spot rate. To see what these extra variables are, one has to consider demands for bonds. Following Frankel (1982, 1983), I take mean–variance optimizing demand functions for, say, DM outside assets (B):

$$B_g / W_g = a_g + b(i - i^* - \Delta s^e) \qquad (36a)$$

$$B_{us} / W_{us} = a_{us} + b(i - i^* - \Delta s^e) \qquad (36b)$$

$$B_{row} / W_{row} = a_{row} + b(i - i^* - \Delta s^e) \qquad (36c)$$

Equation (36a) represents the optimal DM share of German private financial wealth as responding to a constant plus an increasing function of the risk premium. Equation (36b) does the same with reference to US investors and (36c) to the rest of the world. (Presumably $a_g > a_{row} > a_{us}$, due to preferred habitat considerations.) The absence of interest/exchange rates other than the DM's and the dollar's implies that DM and dollar assets are seen as the only ones available for portfolio diversification. I relaxed this restriction by considering a third country's interest rates in the empirical analysis.[8] By simple manipulations of the demand functions (36a, b, c) it is possible to obtain the following reduced form for the DM spot rate:

$$s = -l_0 + l_1(B/W) - l_2(W_g/W) + l_3(W_{us}/W) - (i - i^* - s^e) \qquad (37)$$

where world wealth is $W = W_g + W_{us} + W_{row}$. Note that money supplies may appear in the right-hand side as these are outside assets for the private sector. This way we would obtain a reduced

form *à la* Branson, Halttunen and Masson (1977, 1979). Furthermore, all the other right-hand-side variables from monetary
models could be added to the right-hand side of the reduced form
by replacing uncovered interest parity in the sticky-price monetary model with the risk-premium equation implied by (37).[9] All
said, what the portfolio-balance model does is to add outside assets
and private financial wealth to the determinants of the exchange
rate.

The next section presents empirical results on (combinations of)
the above theoretical models.

EMPIRICAL RESULTS

My empirical analysis used quarterly data, not seasonally adjusted
where possible,[10] from 1973:1 to 1991:4. Dependent variables under
scrutiny are the DM/dollar and yen/dollar exchange rates. Potential explanatory variables are all those included in the reduced
forms of the previous section. My aim was to obtain plausible
equilibrium models, by using cointegration techniques, and subsequently to estimate VARs which are known – thanks to the
Granger representation theorem – to be a legitimate representation of the data generation mechanism when cointegration cannot
be rejected. Subsequently, I applied shocks to the VARs to obtain
impulse response functions which shed light on the relative
sensitivity of the exchange rate to its long-run determinants.

Table 11 details the stochastic properties of the time series at
hand. Clearly, most of them are $I(1)$ with the exception of the
Japanese three-month interest rate (JPTI) which is $I(0)$, M2 (JPM2)
and foreign assets (JPFA) which are $I(2)$. Consequently, most of the
variables can potentially share a long-run relationship with the
appropriate exchange rate.

Let us now turn to the preferred equilibrium model for the
DM/dollar rate. I tested for cointegration through a specific-
to-general approach.[11] This means I started looking for the best
cointegrating couplet, i.e. the DM/dollar rate and the right-hand-
side variable which yields the highest (in absolute value) DF/ADF
test value, while satisfying theoretical priors on expected signs.
The first step in my search showed US private financial wealth
(USWE) as the single best cointegrating variable, yielding

Table 11 Unit root tests on the variables considered*

	I(0)	I(1)	I(2)		I(0)	I(1)	I(2)
DMDL	−1.41	−6.55*		GECA	−2.32	−12.7*	
YEDL	2.98	−6.05*		USPD	0.36	−6.12*	
USM2	1.33	−9.06*		JPPD	−12.1*		
JPM2	2.35	−1.80	−12.1*	GEPD	na	−3.65*	
GEM3	−1.32	−6.81*		USWP	−1.95	−5.24*	
USTI	−2.02	−10.41		JPWP	0.81	−3.46*	
JPCM	−3.80*			GEWP	0.12	−4.07*	
GECM	−1.76	−7.66*		USM3	−1.96	−3.62*	
USBY	−1.98	−6.86*		JPM3	−1.32	−5.03*	
JPBY	−4.08*			JPTI	−3.56*		
GEBY	−1.71	−7.24*		GETI	−2.36	−7.29*	
USRY	−2.40	−5.75*		GEWE	na	−3.22*	
JPRY	1.36	−9.23*		JPWE	na	−3.75*	
GERY	0.53	−8.92*		USWE	na	−5.03*	
USCA	−1.54	−9.04*		GEFA	2.15	−5.82*	
JPCA	−1.32	−8.15*		JPFA	na	−2.03	−8.00*
				USFA	−3.09*		

* Tests are DF or ADF compared against critical values provided in MacKinnon (1991). As suggested by the latter, the tests include a linear trend on the right-hand side whenever the intercept term was significant. An asterisk means the test value is significant at conventional levels. See Appendix 4 for legends; na means autocorrelated residuals even at ADF test level.

an ADF = −4.01. At the second step, I found that German wealth (GEWE) was the best variable to form a cointegrating triplet (ADF = −4.14). I proceeded in this fashion and stopped when adding further right-hand-side variables did not strengthen cointegration. This search uncovered the following equilibrium model:[12]

$$DMDL = 0.022 - 1.38 \times GUWE - 0.055 \times GERI + 0.015 \times USRI \quad (38)$$
$$CRDW = 0.57 \qquad ADF = -4.29$$

Equation (38) says that the DM/dollar rate (DMDL), German private financial wealth relative to the US (GUWE), the German real interest rate (GERI equals bond yield minus current inflation) and its counterpart in the US (USRI) are tied in a long-run relationship. (The restriction embedded in GUWE that the parameter estimates on German and US wealth have the same absolute value was not rejected by the data.) Moreover, note that German outside assets (GEPD) would enter (38) with a coefficient significantly greater than zero, as the portfolio-balance theory predicts. However, GEPD's contribution in terms of 'marginal' cointegration was small and therefore I omitted it from the reported cointegrating equation. Such a long-run model fits a portfolio-balance framework rather than a monetary one. The exchange rate depends on rates of return, outside assets and private financial wealths. Following Frankel (1982, 1983, 1984), private financial wealth is proxied by the sum of public debt outstanding and the cumulated current account balance. In other words, private financial wealth comprises assets which do not net out within one country's private sector.

However, the cointegrating regression (38) was estimated by OLS. While the least-squares approach is simple and intuitive it does, however, suffer from some disadvantages. First, the distribution of cointegration tests like the ADF test will differ slightly in any given application. This reflects the influence of the so-called 'nuisance' parameters (owing to the non-stationarity of the data) in the asymptotic distribution of the coefficient estimates. Second, and more important, any vector of three or more variables (each integrated of the same order) can share more than one cointegrating vector. Indeed, it turns out that if we have a vector of N variables there can be up to $(N-1)$ cointegrating vectors.

Therefore, if OLS estimates do not reject cointegration between three or more variables, there is no assurance to have estimated a unique cointegrating vector. In what follows I check whether this is the case for the previously obtained DM/dollar model. I adopt the Johansen (1988) maximum likelihood method of estimating all of the possible cointegrating vectors. I use the *Microfit* package to solve the so-called eigenvalue problem which Johansen shows as equivalent to maximizing the relevant likelihood function.

Before starting, note that the DM/dollar cointegrating (OLS) regression included a time trend for reasons explained in MacKinnon (1991, p. 269). However, the Johansen approach of estimating VARs in differences cannot accommodate a trend as this would, after differencing, become perfectly collinear with the intercept. Consequently, our starting point is the same set of cointegrating variables apart from the time trend. The OLS estimate of that model is as follows:

$$DMDL = 0.45 - 0.87 \times GUWE - 0.027 \times GERI + 0.029 \times USRI \quad (39)$$
$$CRDW = 0.60 \qquad\qquad\qquad ADF = -4.21$$

The parameters' signs are the same as in (38) although omitting the trend increases the intercept while lowering the absolute value of the GUWE term. The CRDW and ADF values confirm the presumption of cointegration.

The following two tables report the results from the Johansen approach. The likelihood ratio tests in Table 12 suggest that $r = 1$, i.e. there is only one cointegrating vector linking the variables in question. Table 13 shows that the maximum likelihood estimates of the cointegrating parameters are fairly close to the OLS ones reported in equation (39).

Figures 9 and 10 show the results of rolling (OLS) regressions which highlight how the cointegrating parameters evolved through time. It is clear that, throughout the 1980s, the wealth elasticity has been declining in absolute value while that of the (US) interest rate has been growing. This suggests that the degree of substitutability between US and German assets has increased with time. Figure 11 compares the actual values of DMDL against its equilibrium counterparts as estimated by (38). According to my model, in 1991:4 the dollar was undervalued by some 8 per cent

Table 12 Johansen maximum likelihood procedure (non-trended case). Cointegration LR test based on maximal eigenvalue of the stochastic matrix

69 observations from 1974Q4 to 1991Q4. Maximum lag in VAR = 4.

List of variables included in the cointegrating vector:

LDMDL	GUWE	GERI	USRI	Intercept

List of eigenvalues in descending order:

0.38278	0.24554	0.117762	0.038800	0.0000

Null	Alternative	Statistic	95% critical value	90% critical value
$r = 0$	$r = 1$	30.5083	28.1380	25.5590
$r \leq 1$	$r = 2$	14.8524	22.0020	19.7660
$r \leq 2$	$r = 3$	7.0985	15.6720	13.7520
$r \leq 3$	$r = 4$	2.7305	9.2430	7.5250

Table 13 Estimated cointegrated vectors in Johansen estimation
(normalized in brackets)

	69 observations from 1974Q4 to 1991Q4. Maximum lag in VAR = 4, chosen $r = 1$.
	Vector 1
LDMDL	−0.13002
	(−1.0000)
GUWE	−0.11223
	(−0.86317)
GERI	−0.00404
	(−0.03107)
USRI	0.004210
	(0.032380)
Intercept	0.069315
	(0.533110)

against the DM. Interestingly enough, PPP estimates from academics as well as business economists conveyed the same message of dollar undervaluation at the end of 1991.

The next step was to estimate a four-equation VAR from which to derive the impulse response function of DMDL. This is plotted in Figure 12 which shows the change, over sixteen quarters, in the log-level of DMDL following first-period shocks to each of the equations forming the VAR system. (Each shock equals the standard error of the relevant regression.) First, note that the response does not return to zero, which is consistent with the notion of a long-run equilibrium being shocked. Second, the GUWE shock predominates over the interest rate shocks in accord with the relative size of the estimated cointegrating parameters. Third, while the response to GERI's shock has the expected sign, that to USRI's shock does so only for eight quarters to invert thereafter. This could reflect the fact that German interest rates are (partly) determined by the US ones and eventually overreact to USRI shocks. This presumption is confirmed by the impulse response functions of GERI and USRI (see Figures 13 and 14). In fact, GERI's response to a USRI shock accelerates after five quarters while that of USRI to GERI's shock is practically zero. This suggests that German monetary policy is influenced by that

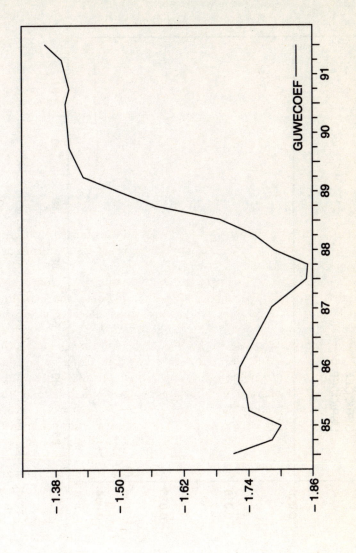

Figure 9 DM/$ model, parameters' evolution (cointegrating regression – relative wealth)

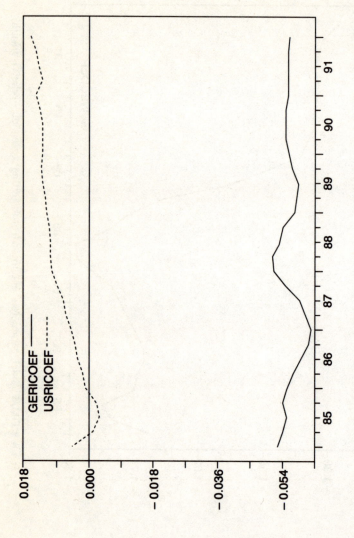

Figure 10 DM/$ model, parameters' evolution (cointegrating regression – real interest rates)

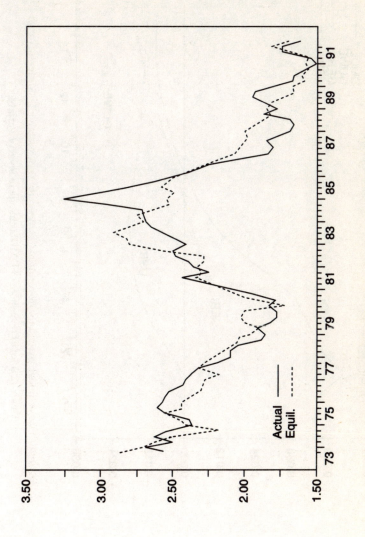

Figure 11 DM/$ model, actual versus equilibrium values

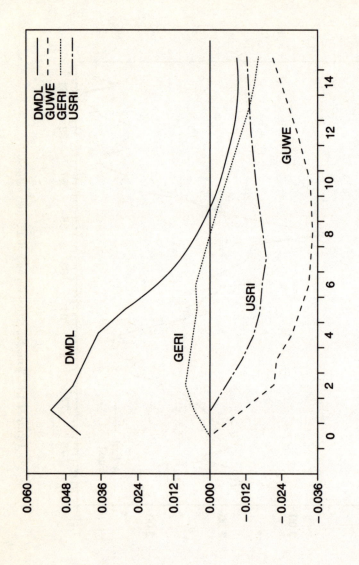

Figure 12 Plot of responses of DMDL: change in level of variable

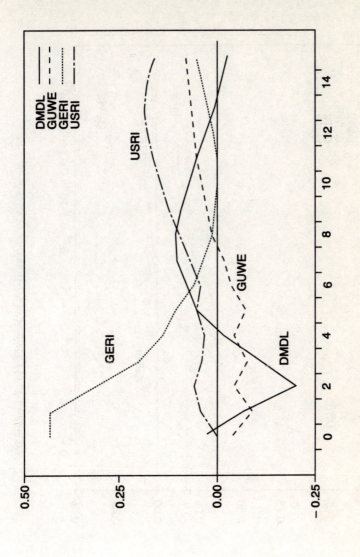

Figure 13 Plot of responses of GERI: change in level of variable

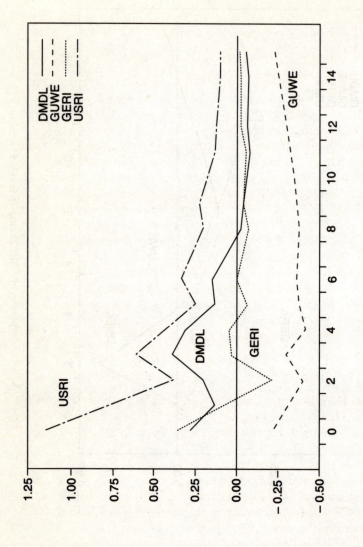

Figure 14 Plot of responses of USRI: change in level of variable

in the US while the latter is driven primarily by domestic considerations.

Let us now turn to modelling the yen/dollar rate. Interestingly enough, the estimated equilibrium relationship is similar to that for the DM/dollar rate. A specific-to-general search led to the following cointegrating regression:

$$\text{YEDL} = 10.58 - 0.99 \times \text{JUWE} - 0.049 \times \text{JUBY} \tag{40}$$
$$\text{CRDW} = 0.49 \qquad \text{ADF} = -4.15$$

Therefore, the portfolio-balance framework seems to tell a reasonable long-run story for the yen/dollar rate too. Note that, similarly to (38), (40) could accommodate outside assets (JPPD) too, yet this would not strengthen the degree of cointegration among the vector's variables. The main difference from the DM/dollar rate is that rates of return here are nominal and not real with the linear cross-country restriction not rejected by the data. As a result, Japanese minus US bond yields (JUBY) appear in the right-hand side. However, note that relative private financial wealth (JUWE) is, as in the DM/dollar model, the predominant long-run determinant.

As with the DM/dollar model, we tested for cointegration also via Johansen's approach. First, equation (41) presents estimates of the long-run model without the time trend on the right-hand side. Relative to (40), removing the trend raises the intercept while lowering the JUWE parameter. The CRDW and ADF statistics remain close to their original values:

$$\text{YEDL} = 13.29 - 1.58 \times \text{JUWE} - 0.055 \times \text{JUBY} \tag{41}$$
$$\text{CRDW} = 0.41 \qquad \text{ADF} = -4.09$$

Table 14 shows there may indeed be one single cointegrating vector. However, the likelihood ratio test value is just below the 95 per cent critical level, thus suggesting that cointegration may not be too strong.

Table 15 shows the maximum likelihood estimates of that cointegrating vector. Again, these are close to the OLS cointegrating estimates of (41), albeit not quite as close as in the DM/dollar case. While these results suggest that the OLS-based analysis is not undermined by multiple cointegrating vectors, they also suggest that the DM/dollar rate may be more successfully modelled than the yen/dollar rate. This was confirmed by my earlier work on

73

Table 14 Johansen maximum likelihood procedure (trended case, no trend in DGP). Cointegration LR test based on maximal eigenvalue of the stochastic matrix

68 observations from 1975Q1 to 1991Q4.
Maximum lag in VAR = 4, chosen $r = 1$.

List of variables included in the cointegrating vector:

LYEDL	JUWE	JUBY

List of eigenvalues in descending order:

0.38038	0.112746	0.039914

Null	Alternative	Statistic	95% critical value	90% critical value
$r = 0$	$r = 1$	20.5283	21.0740	18.9040
$r \leq 1$	$r = 2$	6.6186	14.9000	12.9120
$r \leq 2$	$r = 3$	2.7698	8.1760	6.5000

Table 15 Estimated cointegrated vectors in Johansen estimation (normalized in brackets)

68 observations from 1975Q1 to 1991Q4.
Maximum lag in VAR = 4, chosen $r = 1$.

	Vector 1
LYEDL	1.2525
	(−1.0000)
JUWE	1.8559
	(−1.4818)
JUBY	0.12023
	(−0.09599)
Intercept	14.2682
	(11.3918)

error correction (EC) models. Incidentally, simulating these EC models shows how the DM is more responsive than the yen to changes in rates of return, while the yen is more responsive to current account changes.

Figures 15 and 16 show how the long-run elasticities evolved through time. The wealth elasticity does not show a clear long-run trend although its absolute value has been declining since 1988. The elasticity on the relative interest rate has increased in absolute

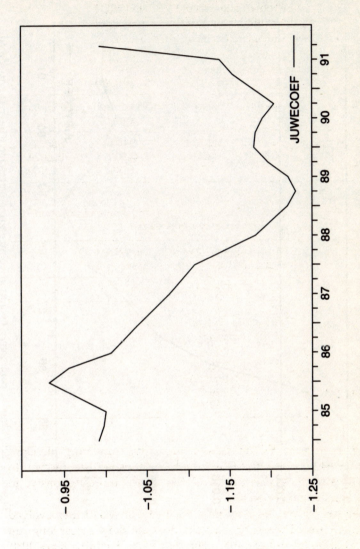

Figure 15 Yen/$ model, parameters' evolution (cointegrating regression – relative wealth)

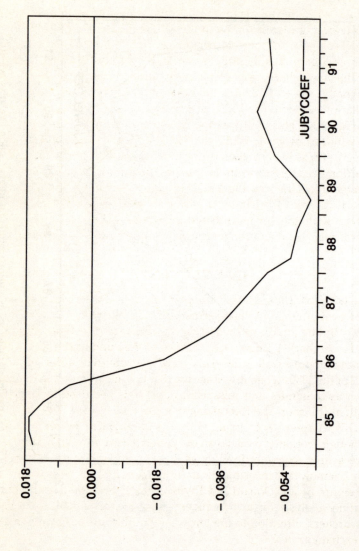

Figure 16 Yen/$ model, parameters' evolution (cointegrating regression – interest rate spread)

value since the mid-1980s. Both these features suggest that, similarly to the DM/dollar case, assets denominated in different currencies have become in time closer substitutes in the eyes of international investors. Figure 17 compares actual yen/dollar values with the long-run equilibrium values estimated by the cointegrating regression. As in the previous case, the dollar looks undervalued – by some 14 per cent at the end of the estimation sample. Again, this message is confirmed by most PPP estimates for the yen/dollar rate available at that time.

Finally, we carried out the VAR-based analysis on the yen/dollar rate as well. The YEDL impulse response function is plotted in Figure 18. This confirms the previous hint that cointegration may indeed be weak. While the YEDL response to a JUWE shock never returns to zero, thus fitting with the notion of a shift from one (long-run) equilibrium to another, the same cannot be said for interest rates. In fact, the YEDL response to a JUBY shock does return to zero, albeit after a period as long as four years. This agrees with the Johansen-based results of Table 14 suggesting 'borderline' cointegration for the yen/dollar model.

CONCLUSIONS

The 1970s saw the success of monetary models of the exchange rate. However, their good times seemed a distant memory by the early 1980s. By the middle of the last decade, conventional wisdom was that asset market models are so deficient they underperform even simple random-walk rules. This view was rebuffed in the second half of the 1980s when it was shown that paying attention to issues such as dynamics and misspecification tests could be rewarded with much improved forecasting models.

This chapter took issue with the late 1980s' wisdom that although economic models can outperform a random-walk rule in forecasting, econometric analyses do not support a unified theory of exchange rate determination. In the previous sections, I have taken up the MacDonald and Taylor (1992) suggestion that cointegration analysis on low-frequency data could help by shifting researchers' attention to the long-run (equilibrium) determinants of exchange rates.

By using quarterly data spanning the last two decades I have

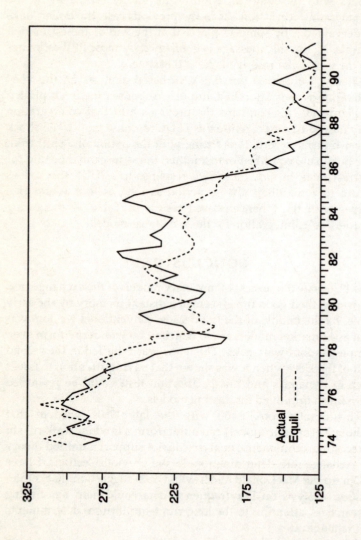

Figure 17 Yen/$ model, actual versus equilibrium values

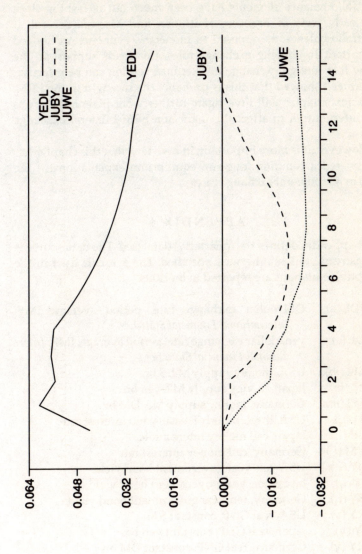

Figure 18 Plot of responses of YEDL: change in level of variable

verified that equilibrium explanations of the DM/dollar and yen/dollar exchange rates can be couched within a portfolio-balance framework which emphasizes financial wealth and outside assets as well as rates of return. This is important for two reasons. First, portfolio-balance elements have been much out of fashion since the early tests of Branson, Halttunen and Masson. Second, if portfolio-balance, as opposed to monetary, elements are indeed important in shaping exchange rates, this lends support to the view that foreign exchange market intervention can be effective. (Chapter 1 showed that this is probably the case within the ERM. The next chapter will investigate further what potential there is for intervention to affect the main non-ERM bilateral exchange rates.)

However, it is more important, in my view, that this chapter has uncovered a common long-run equilibrium explanation for the two major bilateral exchange rates.

APPENDIX 4

This appendix defines the (quarterly) data used. The data source is Datastream, unless otherwise specified. The symbols used in the chapter's equations are reported in brackets.

DMDL (s):	DM/dollar exchange rate, period average, IMF, *International Financial Statistics*.
YEDL (s):	yen/dollar exchange rate, period average, IMF, *International Financial Statistics*.
USM2 (m):	USA, money supply M2, $ bn.
JPM2 (m):	Japan, money supply M2, yen bn.
GEM3 (m):	Germany, money supply M3, DM bn.
USTI (i_s):	USA, three-month Treasury bill interest rate.
JPCM (i_s):	Japan, call money interest rate.
GECM (i_s):	Germany, call money interest rate.
USBY (i_1):	USA, ten-year government bond yield.
JPBY (i_1):	Japan, ten-year government bond yield.
GEBY (i_1):	Germany, ten-year government bond yield.
USRY (y):	USA, real GNP, constant $ bn.
JPRY (y):	Japan, real GDP, constant yen bn.
GERY (y):	Germany, real GNP, constant DM bn.

USCA (CA): USA, current account, $ bn.
JPCA (CA): Japan, current account, $ bn.
GECA (CA): Germany, current account, DM bn.
USPD: USA, public sector debt outstanding, $ bn.
JPPD: Japan, public sector debt outstanding, yen bn.
GEPD: Germany, public sector debt outstanding, DM bn.
USWP (p): USA, wholesale price index.
JPWP (p): Japan, wholesale price index.
GEWP (p): Germany, wholesale price index.
USM3 (m): USA, money supply M3, $ bn.
JPM3 (m): Japan, money supply M3, yen bn.
JPTI (i_s): Japan, three-month Treasury bill interest rate.
GETI (i_s): Germany, three-month interbank interest rate.
GEWE (W_g), JPWE (W_j), USWE (W_{us}): German, Japanese and US private financial wealths, measured in domestic currency. Proxied by adding cumulated current account and public debt outstanding to benchmark values for end-1973 provided by Frankel (1984).
GEFA: Germany, foreign assets, DM bn.
USFA: USA, foreign assets, $ bn.
JPFA: Japan, foreign assets, yen bn.

4

ON THE EFFECTIVENESS
OF FOREIGN EXCHANGE
MARKET INTERVENTION

INTRODUCTION

The empirical analysis in Chapter 3 uncovered a (long-run) link
between major exchange rates and financial wealth, with the latter
partly determined by the stock of outside assets (i.e. public sector
bonds). Can that be taken as evidence of foreign exchange market
intervention being potentially effective via the portfolio-balance
channel? There are at least a couple of problems with such an
interpretation. First, the tests employed in Chapter 3 do not assure
us of the direction of causation between wealth and the exchange
rate. Second, anecdotal evidence is against the possibility that
intervention be used as a long-run means for affecting exchange
rates.

Indeed, it is widely believed that intervention should be used as
a short-run device. Therefore, it would be interesting to check
whether intervention has had, at any time, a short-run causal
effect on exchange rates. The next section brings together issues of
relevance for the interpretation of the empirical results discussed
in the third section. Finally, the last section provides the conclusions.

EARLIER EVIDENCE ON INTERVENTION

Up-to-date and comprehensive reviews on empirical studies of
intervention already exist (see Edison (1990)). Here, I simply
remind the reader of the main conclusions reached while citing
more anecdotal evidence on intervention.

It is fairly widely accepted that unsterilized intervention does affect the exchange rate, but this is simply to say that monetary policy, i.e. changing the money supply and/or interest rates, affects the external value of a currency. Clearly, this is not of much use to the policy maker seeking that extra degree of freedom to decouple (domestic) monetary policy from exchange rate policy. Therefore in what follows, as in Chapter 1, I concentrate on sterilized intervention (from now, simply 'intervention') that leaves interest rates and the monetary base unaffected. Indeed, Edison (1990) reviews evidence that interventions are, in the main, sterilized.

There are basically two channels through which intervention can affect the exchange rate. First, the portfolio-balance channel which exists when outside assets in different currencies are imperfect substitutes in internationally diversified portfolios. Second, the so-called expectations, or signalling channel, when central bankers use intervention as a means to let the market know what they think about currency values.

According to Edison (1990), most studies do not find a quantitatively relevant effect via the first channel, although a few researchers report statistically significant elasticities. However, most studies uncover statistically significant effects of intervention through the expectations/signalling channel. Perhaps the staunchest supporter of the effectiveness of intervention is Dominguez and Frankel (1990), through a two-equation model. The first equation is a mean–variance optimizing inverted bond demand function while the second one models exchange rate expectations – as measured by surveys – via, among others, dummies for (and values of) relevant intervention episodes as announced in the press. Dominguez and Frankel's results are that intervention seems to have a significant effect, both statistically and quantitatively, on exchange rates. This is through both the portfolio-balance and signalling channels. Further prima-facie support for intervention is provided by Belongia's (1992) analysis of daily data on post-1985 periods. The author finds that spells of coordinated intervention by the Federal Reserve System (the Fed) and the Bundesbank, or the Bank of Japan, coincide with significantly larger changes in the DM/dollar and yen/dollar exchange rates.

Kenen (1987) remarks how peculiar it is that the post-1985 period saw exchange rate management gaining favour yet the same did not apply to intervention. Whatever the merits of such a view, it was the legacy of the 1982 Versailles Working Group on intervention. The Group dismissed any usefulness of intervention beyond the day to day horizon. This view was echoed in the Plaza Hotel communiqué of September 1985.

However, despite this official view there is a widespread perception that G7 coordination policy in the second half of the 1980s was no more than a series of campaigns of coordinated foreign exchange market intervention. Gomel, Saccomanni and Vona (1990) identify the spells of more substantial intervention as the following periods:

1   September 1985 to February 1987, with the main central banks trying to correct a perceived dollar overvaluation.
2   February 1987 to June 1988, when the objective was reversed to one of trying to halt a dollar slide.

The subsequent years enjoyed relatively stable exchange rates with external adjustment problems being reduced, thanks to earlier changes in competitiveness and asymmetric national business cycles (i.e. Germany and Japan growing much faster than the USA).

Gaiotti, Giucca and Micossi (1989) present additional stylized facts which help us to interpret the results of the following section. First, apart from the Carter years between 1977 and 1979, intervention by the Fed typically aimed at giving market signals in particular circumstances rather than offering continued market guidance. In other words, the Fed's intervention was typically 'light-weight'. On the contrary, interventions by the Bundesbank and the Bank of Japan tended to be much more continuous. Japanese intervention could be very substantial, on average twice as intense as the Bundesbank's. The Bank of Japan tends to be more active when the dollar weakens, while the Germans intervene more to stem dollar rises for fear of importing inflation. Finally, dollar balances bought (sold) by non-US central banks are usually reinvested (withdrawn from) in the USA. In other words, the US monetary base is automatically sterilized without the Fed having to do so. On the other hand, the Bank of Japan and the Bundesbank often claim to pursue sterilization and this is confirmed econometrically by 'offset' coefficient estimates typically close to minus one.[1]

DIRECT TESTS ON INTERVENTION

Only in very few cases have researchers uncovered a systematic effect from intervention to the exchange rate – more often than not in studies of the portfolio-balance channel. For instance, Dominguez and Frankel (1990) find some support for such a channel affecting the DM/dollar rate, against many previously unsuccessful attempts (see e.g. Rogoff (1984)). Chapter 1 shows that evidence for such a channel is more readily available from the ERM foreign exchange markets.

However, these studies beg two crucial interrelated questions. What is the direction of causation: that is, are exchange rates affected by the supply of assets or do they affect asset demands (with supply passively adjusting)? This limitation reflects only partly the use of reduced forms. Second, is such a portfolio-balance channel, assuming it exists, actually exploited to affect exchange rates?[2] Here I present some more direct evidence on causality and, whenever this allows us to proceed further, on the actual impact of intervention on exchange rates.

The empirical analysis adopts a methodology originally proposed by Adams and Henderson (1983). It is well known that when assembling data to represent exchange market intervention one encounters institutional obstacles that preclude extracting the effect of intervention. (Non-sterilized intervention can be simply approximated by changes in official reserves.) The method adopted here approximates the desired information by 'augmenting' conventionally reported data.

Remember that sterilized intervention leaves the monetary liabilities of both the domestic and foreign central bank unchanged. In other words, an intervention operation is equivalent to a trade in domestic securities for foreign ones. Those stock changes affect the monetary authorities' balance sheets which are, therefore, helpful in analysing intervention. A stylized balance sheet looks as follows:

ASSETS	*LIABILITIES*
Net domestic assets	Monetary liabilities
Net foreign assets	Net worth

Following Adams and Henderson (1983), 'intervention operations

... can be represented by changes in the ... balance sheet. An intervention ... involves offsetting changes in net foreign assets and net domestic ones (dNFA = −dNDA) and no changes in either monetary liabilities or net worth (dML = dNW = 0)'. To identify the effect of intervention on exchange rates one needs data on three of the four balance sheet items. Then the following equation can be estimated:

$$dE = a_0 + a_1 dNFA + a_2 dML + a_3 dNW + a_4 dX \qquad (42)$$

where X can be one or more extra variables in order to reduce omitted-variable bias. The estimate of a_1 would then be the elasticity of the exchange rate with respect to intervention. Indeed, that would be the effect of sterilized intervention thanks to the *ceteris paribus* property that dML = dNW = 0. Luckily, monthly data on central bank balance sheets are available from the *International Financial Statistics* of the IMF.[3]

However, standard estimation of (42) begs once again the question of the direction of causality. That was highlighted by preliminary OLS estimates in which a_1 turned out to be significantly negative, thus implying that central bank purchases of foreign securities boost the exchange rate. (Empirically, that was measured by the i/SDR bilateral rate, with i = dollar, DM, yen, franc, lira.) Clearly, a_1 ought to be positive if intervention works.

To shed light on the simultaneity issue we carried out causality tests between NFA and E prior to estimating (42). We employed the Granger and Sims causality tests. Consider the following equation:

$$Y_t = \sum_{j=-\infty}^{\infty} b_j X_{t-j} \qquad (43)$$

where $b_j = 0$ for all $j < 0$ if and only if Y fails to Granger-cause X (see Sims (1972)). The Granger test regresses Y on the lagged Y and the lagged X and tests the significance of the lags of X. The Sims test regresses X on the past, present and future Y and tests the leads of Y. Since causality tests may lack power, using both versions should help. Moreover, I ran each test both ways, i.e. I did both causality and reverse-causality tests seeking internally consistent answers.[4] These are contained in Table 16.

Reassuringly, it is clear from the table that the Granger and Sims

Table 16 Causality tests between intervention and exchange rates[a]

Sample periods		1974–91	1974–9	1980–5	1986–91	Equation estimation results
Granger	Causality	3.43 (0.01**)	0.22 (0.92)	2.28 (0.07*)	3.06 (0.02**)	OLS: coefficient on
($)	Reverse	3.18 (0.01**)	2.17 (0.08*)	0.56 (0.69)	3.99 (0.06*)	ΔNFA = 0
Sims	Causality	2.42 (0.05**)	0.38 (0.82)	1.17 (0.32)	2.85 (0.03**)	IV: coefficient on
($)	Reverse	3.31 (0.0**)	2.15 (0.08*)	1.04 (0.39)	4.0 (0.01**)	ΔNFA = 0 (result
Intervention causes $?		Two-way causation	No; $ causes NFA	No	Two-way causation	holds also after adding more behavioural variables)
Granger	Causality	0.31 (0.87)	0.79 (0.53)	0.73 (0.57)	0.47 (0.78)	OLS: coefficient on
(DM)	Reverse	1.82 (0.12)	0.80 (0.53)	1.15 (0.34)	0.40 (0.81)	ΔNFA = −0.13
Sims	Causality	0.25 (0.91)	0.91 (0.46)	0.67 (0.61)	0.46 (0.76)	IV: coefficient on
(DM)	Reverse	1.66 (0.16)	0.78 (0.54)	1.41 (0.24)	0.28 (0.89)	ΔNFA = −0.20
Intervention causes DM?		No	No	No	No	(adding behav-ioural variables makes it = 0)
Granger	Causality	0.11 (0.98)	1.84 (0.13)	0.07 (0.99)	1.51 (0.21)	OLS: coefficient on
(yen)	Reverse	0.17 (0.95)	3.62 (0.01**)	0.10 (0.98)	0.55 (0.70)	ΔNFA = −0.06
Sims	Causality	0.10 (0.98)	1.53 (0.21)	0.07 (0.99)	1.54 (0.20)	IV: coefficient on
(yen)	Reverse	0.17 (0.95)	3.49 (0.01**)	0.10 (0.98)	0.33 (0.85)	ΔNFA = 0 (also after
Intervention causes yen?		No	No; yen causes NFA	No	No	adding more behavioural vari-ables)
Granger	Causality	0.55 (0.70)	2.23 (0.08*)	0.35 (0.84)	0.98 (0.42)	OLS: coefficient on
(franc)	Reverse	0.45 (0.77)	0.96 (0.44)	0.50 (0.74)	0.17 (0.95)	ΔNFA = 0
Sims	Causality	0.61 (0.66)	2.26 (0.07*)	0.38 (0.83)	0.75 (0.56)	(same result with
(franc)	Reverse	0.54 (0.70)	1.32 (0.27)	0.47 (0.76)	0.37 (0.83)	IV and more
Intervention causes franc?		No	Yes (?)	No	No	behavioural variables)
Granger	Causality	0.13 (0.97)	0.79 (0.54)	0.55 (0.70)	2.13 (0.09*)	OLS: coefficient on
(lira)	Reverse	0.09 (0.98)	0.16 (0.96)	0.53 (0.71)	1.36 (0.26)	ΔNFA = 0
Sims	Causality	0.13 (0.97)	0.57 (0.69)	1.22 (0.31)	1.92 (0.12)	(same result with
(lira)	Reverse	0.27 (0.90)	0.27 (0.90)	0.35 (0.84)	0.75 (0.56)	IV and more
Intervention causes lira?		No	No	No	Yes (?)	behavioural variables)

a Exchange rates are *vis-à-vis* the SDR. All data are monthly. Granger tests use lags up to (t–4). Sims' tests include leads up to (t+4). The tests' statistics follow an *F* distribution; tests' significance levels are in parentheses. * = null of no causation rejected at the 95% level. ** = null of no causation rejected at the 90% level. NFA = central bank's net foreign assets tests do not give conflicting answers. The causality results refer to each of the five exchange rates *vis-à-vis* the SDR, both for the whole floating period and three sub-samples. For the sake of brevity, the results from estimating (42), by OLS and IV, refer to the whole sample. The estimation results, especially those by IV, are consistent with the prior evidence of the causality tests.

In a nutshell, I never find evidence that intervention systematically determines the three main exchange rates (dollar, DM and yen). This agrees with the negative inference from much of the literature surveyed by Edison (1990). (However, it is still possible that intervention is effective in the shorter term and this can only be detected by higher-frequency data.) Much the same goes for the two ERM currencies considered, the lira and franc. Only on the lira is there some evidence (from the Granger test) that intervention had an impact. On the ERM currencies, the results are less supportive of intervention than those in Chapter 1. However, this may be due to the fact that here I use effective as opposed to bilateral exchange rates. As a result, the effect of ERM intervention is diluted in the wider model used here.

CONCLUSIONS

This chapter has taken stock of the existing empirical studies on foreign exchange market intervention, concluding that there is, at best, scant evidence in its favour. However, the vast majority of tests begs the crucial question of causality between central bank net foreign assets and the exchange rate. (This pitfall undermines reduced-form exchange rate determination models as well.)

I have examined this issue by taking up the Adams and Henderson (1983) methodology of using data from central bank balance sheets to proxy sterilized intervention. Extensive causality tests on the three main currencies confirm that intervention has not had a systematic influence on those currencies, at least not on monthly data. (However, remember Belongia's (1992) prima-facie evidence, from daily data, in support of intervention – see the second section.) There are hints of some effects on the lira but the implications for ERM intervention are weaker than those from Chapter 1, partly because here effective exchange rates are used instead of bilateral ERM rates.

CONCLUSIONS

The motivating aim of this book was to assess the relative efficacy of alternative means of curbing exchange rate volatility. The evidence presented in the previous four chapters suggests the following. First, coordinated monetary policies, especially seen as affecting real interest rates, are almost always an effective way to steer exchange rates. Second, (sterilized) intervention is probably quite effective in affecting exchange rates such as those of EMS currencies *vis-à-vis* the DM. However, intervention alone is doomed to be ineffective at times of strong speculative attacks. Third, capital and foreign exchange controls are eventually circumvented, i.e. they become ineffective in the long run. Fourth, despite evidence of portfolio-balance influences on the DM/dollar and yen/dollar rates, there is only feeble evidence that intervention has systematically affected the main exchange rates outside the EMS.

The first chapter took issue with the view, fashionable in the late 1980s, that capital controls were necessary in keeping the ERM functioning. The work presented there shows the balance of evidence being in favour of intramarginal intervention and convergence of monetary policies. Indeed, a simple reflection suggests that the importance of controls had been overrated. During the 1970s, European capital controls were no laxer than in the 1980s, yet exchange rate volatility was much higher. Something quite apart from controls must have laid behind the reduced (intra-ERM) exchange rate volatility of the last decade. The first chapter presents evidence in favour of ERM exchange rate risk premia which depend (also) on outside assets. As such, there is a role for intervention to affect ERM parities as witnessed by the increasing recourse to intramarginal intervention. Indeed, events following the late 1980s' liberalization confirmed Chapter 1's prediction that capital controls were not the key to the success of the ERM. (The realignments of 1992 reflected the timing of the referenda on the Treaty of Maastricht. That gave speculators target dates around which to concentrate attacks against weaker ERM currencies. Given our results on the long-run ineffectiveness of capital controls there are reasons to believe the realignments would have occurred even had controls been maintained in force.)

Chapter 2 took that theme further by quantifying the impact on French and Italian official reserves of capital and foreign exchange controls. My empirical results suggest that those controls were effective only for a few years following the inception of the EMS in 1979. It seems that controls ceased to bite by 1985. Given that, it is no surprise that the ERM withstood successfully the removal of Italian and French capital controls in 1989–90. However, the short-run (as opposed to long-run) insulating properties of controls would have helped the ERM authorities to counter the 1992–3 currency turbulence with more timely realignments, thus avoiding presenting foreign exchange speculators with one-way bets.

Chapter 3 built upon earlier work indicating that monetary models of the exchange rate, albeit not fully supported by the data, can easily (if properly estimated) outperform random-walk models in forecasting. That earlier work concluded that perhaps portfolio-balance elements should be re-examined. Indeed, Chapter 3 showed that outside assets and real rates of return adequately capture the equilibrium determinants of the main exchange rates. Does this mean that sterilized intervention can affect the main currencies as well as the ERM's? Not really.

The direct tests on intervention presented in Chapter 4 show that intervention does not systematically Granger-cause exchange rates (at least not on monthly data). As a result, it seems that the link unveiled in Chapter 3 between financial wealth and exchange rates owes more to the cumulation of private sector's foreign assets than to outside assets. In other words, the main currencies are affected by long-run sustainability conditions on external debt as well as real rates of return.

NOTES

INTRODUCTION

1   Policy coordination was tried both at the G5 level (the period between the Plaza Accord of September 1985 and the Louvre Agreement in February 1987) and within Europe through the ERM.
2   The 'ERM-induced' constant exchange rate rule coupled with the low-inflation goal of Germany, the 'dominant' country, means that other members' monetary policies are prevented from fine tuning demand.
3   These are fairly conventional and ignore modelling issues brought up by the literature on target zones and non-linearities. In this respect we note, however, that Flood, Rose and Mathieson (1990) and Meese and Rose (1989, 1990) conclude that little empirical advantage is gained by working with non-linear, rather than more conventional, models.

1 ERM STABILITY, CAPITAL CONTROLS AND FOREIGN EXCHANGE MARKET INTERVENTION

1   The view that the ERM had stood together mainly thanks to capital controls is shared, for instance, by Rogoff (1985) and Goodhart (1986).
2   Volatility interpreted as 'forecastability' may be more relevant to micro agents than to national economies. Micro agents are interested in forecastability of exchange rates since unpredictability can be offset through hedging instruments. National economies are more interested in (real) volatility because this affects export competitiveness, and hence output and employment.
3   For instance, the McKinnon (1982) proposal of controlling the world money supply also aims at stabilizing exchange rates. Yet such a form of cooperation would not necessarily show up in higher correlations between national money supplies. This is because these should be targeted to accommodate money demand shifts from one currency to another.
4   One could contrast the German monetary discipline throughout the

period with the French abrupt change in monetary policy which accompanied the advent of the socialist government, or with the repeated overshoots of intermediate targets of monetary policy (total domestic credit) in Italy.

5 See e.g. Rogoff (1985) and Goodhart (1986).

6 For further details on this point, see Micossi (1985).

7 For example, when real as opposed to nominal shocks hit the system. See Henderson (1984).

8 Interventions relying on the VSTFF have such a property. The perceived effectiveness of preventive intramarginal intervention prompted some central banks to advocate extending the use of the VSTFF to finance that kind of intervention too. Such change was initially resisted by the Bundesbank, reflecting the desire to maintain full control over its monetary base.

9 Interventions in dollars (and other non-EMS currencies) were probably intramarginal given the impossibility, until September 1987, of drawing on the VSTFF to finance intramarginal intervention. Further evidence supporting the role of intramarginal interventions can be found in the Report of the Deutsche Bundesbank for the year 1987, p. 68.

10 In what follows, I assume that central banks sterilize the effect of foreign exchange market interventions on their monetary bases.

11 Some researchers have also tried to allow for the existence of *ex post* bias in the forward exchange rate without requiring the presence of outside assets. However, testing for the risk premium along these lines requires one to consider models not amenable to conventional estimation. On this point, see Boothe and Longworth (1986).

12 Preliminary estimates on (5) using monthly average data on Italy–Germany yielded 'significant' $\hat{\alpha} < 0$, $\hat{\beta} > 0$, thus rejecting the null hypothesis of perfect assets substitutability.

13 Attempts with alternative dynamic specifications proved unsuccessful. The residuals' correlogram showed mainly a first-order autocorrelation problem. Therefore, we tried to cope by including among the regressors also the lagged dependent variable and/or first (and second) lag on the explanatory variable, thus assuming in turn partial adjustment, geometric lag on (A/SA^*) and AR(1) residuals. In any event, assuming adjustment lags on the Euromarkets would be theoretically unappealing.

14 Assuming – as is customary – that the spot rate is the 'jump' variable which accommodates changes in the risk premium.

15 Different monetary authorities are likely to rely on different models of the economy and have different macroeconomic goals.

16 All variables are in logarithms.

17 The F test for $\hat{\alpha}_1$ stability tells us that the null hypothesis cannot be rejected for Japan only.

18 Frankel (1983) shows that given an asset share demand function of the type $a + b(RP)$ (where RP = risk premium), $a = \alpha[f(\rho)]$. α is the weight of foreign goods in the consumer's utility function, whilst ρ is the coefficient of relative risk aversion. Therefore, assuming equal risk aversion at home and abroad, $\varphi_0 > 0$ (in (A.6)) as long as the weight of foreign goods in the consumers' utility function is greater at home than abroad.

2 THE EFFECTIVENESS OF CAPITAL CONTROLS: AN EMPIRICAL ANALYSIS OF THE ERM

1 In the remainder of the chapter, the term controls will embrace both capital and foreign exchange controls.

2 Adams and Greenwood (1985) show dual exchange rates to be generally equivalent to other capital controls. However, equivalence breaks down if controls are not perfect, thus allowing some amount of private arbitrage to take place. Gros (1988) shows that conditions which arouse private arbitrage are more easily met under dual exchange rates than under other forms of controls.

3 And also if, as suggested by numerical analyses in Mendoza (1989), the welfare loss is empirically small.

4 Such evidence refers to the volatility of Eurofranc and Eurolira interest rates converging towards that of the corresponding onshore rates.

5 For instance, Obstfeld (1986a) presents a growth model where changes in population make saving and investment rates move in close fashion.

6 Or inequalities between onshore and offshore interest rates.

7 Covered arbitrage focuses on $[(1 + i)/(1 + i^*) - F/S]$, covered speculation on F/S and uncovered arbitrage on $[(1 + i)/(1 + i^*) - S^e/S]$; where $i =$ domestic interest rate, $i^* =$ foreign interest rate, $S =$ spot price of foreign currency in terms of domestic currency, $S^e =$ expected future spot rate, $F =$ forward price of foreign currency in terms of domestic currency.

8 Although both countries aimed at curbing outflows rather than inflows, the latter may be costly too. In the case of repatriation of illegally exported funds there is the danger of arousing the authorities' suspicion, whilst for foreigners investing in France or Italy the cost lies with the probability of difficult repatriation of funds.

9 Again, I rely on the (empirically verified) assumption that the expression in the last square brackets of equation (23) follows an AR(1) process with τ as the autoregressive parameter.

10 SE is intended as units of foreign currency for domestic currency (i.e. an increase means appreciation and vice versa), in conformity with the usual criterion of compilation for effective exchange rates.

11 That is, below the level dictated by uncovered interest parity.

12 The Gauss–Newton algorithm was applied which is identical to the ML estimator if the residuals are normally distributed – see Harvey (1981, p. 95).

13 Note that Switzerland, an important destination for illegal capital from both France and Italy, can be subsumed under Germany given the collinearity between movements in the DM and the Swiss franc, and between German and Swiss interest rates.

14 Chiefly, the lifting of a previous ban on the use of credit cards abroad, the abolition of a tax on investments in foreign bonds and a lowering to 75 per cent of the proportion of direct investment (towards the EC area) to be financed via foreign borrowing.

15 The order i of the polynomial was chosen so as to minimize the regression's standard error.

16 Call RP^* the 'risk-premium' term attached to σ_i and RP the risk premium $[(1 + i_t)/(1 + i_t^*) - S_{t+1}^c/S_t]$ entering standard bond demand functions. Then the value of σ_i consistent with high capital mobility – i.e. no controls – may be obtained by solving $\sigma_i . RP^* = qRP$ where q is the elasticity of bond demand with respect to expected return in the high-mobility case. We gave q the value of 0.044, deduced from table 7 in Danker et $al.$ (1985) which presents estimates of risk-premium equations for the Germany–USA case.

17 The previous chapter provided evidence that sterilized foreign exchange market intervention was another factor supporting the lira.

18 As done for instance in Dooley and Isard (1980) and Claassen and Wyplosz (1982).

3 EXCHANGE RATE DETERMINATION: MONETARY OR PORTFOLIO-BALANCE EFFECTS?

1 Comprehensive reviews can be found in Isard (1986) and MacDonald and Taylor (1992).

2 On this, one inevitably quotes the well-known Meese and Rogoff (1983a, b, 1985) papers which sanctioned the superiority of a random-walk rule in forecasting exchange rates.

3 Forecasting tests are not carried out as the emphasis here is on explaining the long-run forces shaping exchange rates. Therefore, I implicitly concede there is little scope for short-term forecasting with structural models.

4 Lower-case variables are in logarithms, apart from interest rates. The algebraic signs preceding parameters are those expected on theoretical grounds. An asterisk next to a variable means it refers to the foreign country. Variables' legends are listed in Appendix 4.

5 Clearly, this formalization would be improper were central banks' interventions in the foreign exchange market relevant. In such a case, Δres ought to be determined by a policy reaction function.

6 A more appropriate formulation including expectations would see the last term in (33) amended as follows: $f_3(i_s - i_s^* - \Delta s^e)$. However, by assuming rational expectations the model's solution would still look like (34) – see appendix 1 to Radaelli (1988).

7 Out of the many formulations available, I favour that proposed in Frankel (1982, 1983).

8 Japan was taken as the 'third country' in modelling the DM/dollar

rate while Germany took that role in modelling the yen/dollar rate.

9   Such synthesis of monetary and portfolio-balance models was proposed in Frankel (1984, p. 25).

10 The impact of seasonal dummies always proved insignificantly different from zero.

11 This was preferred to the customary (in dynamic regression models) general-to-specific approach because the power of cointegration tests declines as the number of (possibly) cointegrating variables increases.

12 Note that the cointegration regressions include a linear trend for reasons detailed in MacKinnon (1991, p. 269).

4 ON THE EFFECTIVENESS OF FOREIGN EXCHANGE MARKET INTERVENTION

1   Formally, if DC = domestic credit and NFA = net foreign assets, α tends to take the value -1 in estimates of $dDC = \alpha dNFA + \ldots$.

2   Chapter 1 attempts to provide an answer for ERM parities.

3   Admittedly, daily or weekly data would be preferable. As a result, negative results from my estimates still leave open the possibility that intervention may be effective, but only within the space of a few days or weeks.

4   The causality tests were preceded by cointegration tests to ascertain whether causality should be tested on levels or first differences. Engle and Granger (1987) show that in the presence of cointegration between the level of variables it is wrong to run causality tests on differenced data – levels ought to be used instead. This is because, under cointegration, an error correction model exists and this can be reparameterized as a VAR in levels but not in first differences (the level-form error correction term would be left out by the differenced representation).

REFERENCES

Adams, Charles and Greenwood, Jeremy (1985), Dual Exchange Rate Systems and Capital Controls: An Introduction, *Journal of International Economics*, 18, pp. 43–63.

Adams, Donald B. and Henderson, Dale W. (1983), Definition and Measurement of Exchange Market Intervention, Board of Governors of the Federal Reserve System, *Staff Studies*, no. 126, September.

Artis, M. J. (1986), External Aspects of the EMS, paper presented at the SUERF Colloquium, Luxembourg, October.

Backus, David (1984), Empirical Models of the Exchange Rate: Separating the Wheat from the Chaff, *Canadian Journal of Economics*, 17, 4, pp. 824–46.

Begg, D. K. H. (1982), *The Rational Expectations Revolution in Macroeconomics, Theories and Evidence*, Oxford: Philip Allan.

Belongia, Michael T. (1992), Foreign Exchange Intervention by the United States: A Review and Assessment of 1985–89, *The Federal Reserve Bank of St Louis Review*, vol. 74, 3, May/June.

Bilson, John F. O. (1978a), The Monetary Approach to the Exchange Rate: Some Empirical Evidence, *IMF Staff Papers*, 25, March, pp. 48–75.

―――― (1978b), Rational Expectations and the Exchange Rate, chapter 5 in Frenkel, Jacob A. and Johnson, Harry (eds), *The Economics of the Exchange Rate: Selected Studies*, Reading, Massachusetts, pp. 75–96.

―――― (1978c), The DM/dollar Rate: A Monetary Analysis, *Carnegie–Mellon Conference Series on Public Policy*, pp. 59–101.

Bini Smaghi, L. and Vona, S. (1987), The Effects of Economic Convergence and Competitiveness on Trade Among the EMS Countries, in Hodgman, D. and Woods, J. (eds), *Macroeconomic Policy and Economic Interdependence*, London: Macmillan Press.

Black, S. W. (1976), Comment on J. Williamson, 'Exchange Rate Flexibility and Reserves Use', *Scandinavian Journal of Economics*, pp. 340–5.

Boothe, P. and Longworth, D. (1986), Foreign Exchange Market Efficiency Tests: Implications of Recent Empirical Findings, *Journal of International Money and Finance*, June, pp. 135–52.

REFERENCES

Branson, William, Halttunen, Hannu and Masson, Paul (1977), Exchange Rates in the Short Run: The DM/dollar Rate, *European Economic Review*, 10, December, pp. 303–24.

—— (1979), Exchange Rates in the Short Run: Some Further Results, *European Economic Review*, 12, October, pp. 395–402.

Buiter, W. H. and Miller, M. (1981), Monetary Policy and International Competitiveness: The Problems of Adjustment, *Oxford Economic Papers*, September, pp. 143–75.

Claassen, Emil-Maria and Wyplosz, Charles (1982), Capital Controls: Some Principles and the French Experience, *Annales de l'Insee*, pp. 47–8, 237–67.

Cody, Brian (1989), Imposing Exchange Controls to Dampen Currency Speculation: Political Risk and the French Franc, 1976–1984, *European Economic Review*, 33, pp. 1751–68.

Cumby, R. E., Huizinga, J. and Obstfeld, M. (1983), Two-step, Two-stage Least Squares Estimation in Models with Rational Expectations, *Journal of Econometrics*, March, pp. 333–55.

Cushman, D. B. (1983), The Effects of Exchange Rate Risk on International Trade, *Journal of International Economics*, December, pp. 403–29.

Danker, Deborah, Haas, Richard A., Henderson, Dale W., Symansky, Steven A. and Tyron, Ralph (1985), Small Empirical Models of Exchange Market Intervention: Applications to Germany, Japan and Canada, Board of Governors of the Federal Reserve System, *Staff Studies*, no. 135.

Dominguez, Kathryn Mary and Frankel, Jeffrey (1990), Does Foreign Exchange Intervention Matter? Disentangling the Portfolio and Expectations Effect for the Mark, *NBER Working Paper*, no. 3299, March.

Dooley, Michael P. and Isard, Peter (1980), Capital Controls, Political Risk, and Deviations from Interest-rate Parity, *Journal of Political Economy*, 88, 2, pp. 370–84.

Dornbusch, Rudiger (1976), Expectations and Exchange Rate Dynamics, *Journal of Political Economy*, 84, December, pp. 1161–76.

—— (1980), Exchange Rate Economics: Where Do We Stand?, *Brookings Papers on Economic Activity*, 1, pp. 143–85.

—— (1986), Flexible Exchange Rates and Excess Capital Mobility, *Brookings Papers on Economic Activity*, 1, pp. 209–26.

Driffill, John (1988), The Stability and Sustainability of the European Monetary System with Perfect Capital Markets, in Giavazzi, F., Micossi, S. and Miller, M. (eds), *The European Monetary System*, Cambridge University Press, pp. 211–28.

Driskill, Robert A. (1981), Exchange Rate Dynamics: An Empirical Investigation, *Journal of Political Economy*, 89, April, pp. 357–71.

EC Commission (1988), *European Economy*, no. 36, May.

Edison, Hali J. (1990), Foreign Currency Operations: An Annotated Bibliography, *International Finance Discussion Papers*, no. 380, May.

Edwards, Sebastian (1989), *Real Exchange Rates, Devaluation and Adjustment*, MIT Press.

100

REFERENCES

Engle, Robert F. and Granger, Clive W. J. (1987), Cointegration and Error Correction: Representation, Estimation and Testing, *Econometrica*, 55, March, pp. 251–76.

Feldstein, Martin S. and Horioka, Charles (1980), Domestic Savings and International Capital Flows, *Economic Journal*, 90, June, pp. 314–29.

Flood, Robert P., Rose, Andrew K. and Mathieson, Donald J. (1990), 'Is the EMS the Perfect Fix? An Empirical Exploration of Exchange Rate Target Zones', *International Finance Discussion Papers*, no. 388, October.

Frankel, Jeffrey (1979), On the Mark: A Theory of Floating Exchange Rates Based on Real Interest Differentials, *American Economic Review*, 69, September, pp. 610–22.

—— (1982), A Test of Perfect Substitutability in the Foreign Exchange Market, *Southern Economic Journal*, October, pp. 406–16.

—— (1983), Estimation of Portfolio-balance Functions that are Mean-variance Optimising: The Mark and the Dollar, *European Economic Review*, pp. 315–27.

—— (1984), Tests of Monetary and Portfolio-balance Models of Exchange Rate Determination, chapter 7 in Bilson, John and Marston, Richard (eds), *Exchange Rate Theory and Practice*, University of Chicago Press, pp. 239–60.

Frenkel, Jacob A. (1976), A Monetary Approach to the Exchange Rate: Doctrinal Aspects and Empirical Evidence, *Scandinavian Journal of Economics*, 78, pp. 200–24.

Gaiotti, E., Giucca, P. and Micossi, Stefano (1989), Cooperation in Managing the Dollar (1985–87): Interventions in Foreign Exchange Markets and Interest Rates, Banca d'Italia, *Temi di Discussione*, no. 119, June.

Galy, M. (1984), An Empirical Evaluation of the Monetary Integration Process within EMS Members, Presented at the Conference: The EMS: Policy Coordination and Exchange Rate Systems, Manchester, September.

Giavazzi, F. and Giovannini, A. (1986), Capital Controls and the EMS, paper presented at the SUERF Colloquium, Luxembourg, October.

Giavazzi, Francesco and Giovannini, Alberto (1989), *Limiting Exchange Rate Flexibility: The European Monetary System*, MIT Press.

Giavazzi, Francesco and Pagano, Marco (1985), Capital Controls and the European Monetary System, *Euromobiliare*, Occasional Paper.

Giavazzi, Francesco and Spaventa, Luigi (1990), The 'New' EMS, *CEPR Discussion Paper*, no. 369, January.

Gomel, G., Saccomanni, F. and Vona, S. (1990), The Experience with Economic Policy Coordination: The Tripolar and European Dimensions, Banca d'Italia, *Temi di Discussione*, no. 140, July.

Goodhart, C. (1986), Has the Time Come for the UK to Join the EMS? *The Banker*, February, pp. 26–8.

Gordon, David B. and Levine, Ross (1988), The Capital Flight 'Problem', Board of Governors of the Federal Reserve System, *International Finance Discussion Papers*, no. 320, April.

Greenwood, Jeremy and Kimbrough, Kim P. (1985), Capital Controls and Fiscal Policy in the World Economy, *Canadian Journal of Economics*, 18, 743–65.

Gros, Daniel (1987), The Effectiveness of Capital Controls – Implications for Monetary Autonomy in the Presence of Incomplete Market Separation, *IMF Staff Papers*, December, pp. 621–42.

―――― (1988), Dual Exchange Rates in the Presence of Incomplete Market Separation – Long Run Effectiveness and Policy Implications, *IMF Staff Papers*, September, pp. 437–62.

Harvey, A. C. (1981), *The Econometric Analysis of Time Series*, Oxford: Philip Allan.

Henderson, D. W. (1984), Exchange Market Intervention Operations: Their Role in Financial Policy and their Effects, in Bilson, J. and Marston, M. (eds), *Exchange Rate Theory and Practice*, University of Chicago Press, pp. 359–406.

Hooper, Peter and Morton, John (1982), Fluctuations in the Dollar: A Model of Nominal and Real Exchange Rate Determination, *Journal of International Money and Finance*, 1, April, pp. 39–56.

Isard, Peter (1986), Alternative Approaches to Empirical Modelling of Exchange Rates: Where is the Profession Now?, mimeo, Brookings Institution, March.

IMF (1984), Exchange Rate Volatility and World Trade, *Occasional Paper*, no. 28.

Johansen, S. (1988), Statistical Analysis of Cointegrating Vectors, *Journal of Economic Dynamics and Control*, 12, pp. 231–54.

Johnson, Harry G. (1969), Theoretical Problems of the International Monetary System, in Cooper, R. N. (ed.), *International Finance*, Penguin.

Kenen, Peter B. (1987), Exchange Rate Management: What Role for Intervention?, *American Economic Review, Papers and Proceedings*, pp. 194–9, May.

MacDonald, Ronald and Taylor, Mark (1992), Exchange Rate Economics: A Survey, *IMF Staff Papers*, March, pp. 1–58.

McKinnon, I. (1982), Currency Substitution and Instability in the World Dollar Standard, *American Economic Review*, June, pp. 321–33.

MacKinnon, James (1991), Critical Values for Cointegration Tests, in Engle, R. F. and Granger, Clive J. (eds), *Long-run Economic Relationships*, Oxford University Press, pp. 238–66.

Masera, S. (1986), An Increasing Role for the ECU: A Character in Search of a Script, Banca d'Italia, *Temi di Discussione*, June.

Meese, Richard A. and Rogoff, Kenneth (1983a), Empirical Exchange Rate Models of the Seventies: Do they Fit out of Sample?, *Journal of International Economics*, 14, February, pp. 3–24.

―――― (1983b), The Out-of-sample Failure of Empirical Exchange Rate Models: Sampling Error or Misspecification?, in Frankel, Jacob (ed.), *Exchange Rates and International Macroeconomics*, University of Chicago Press, pp. 67–105.

REFERENCES

—— (1985), Was it Real? The Exchange Rate–Interest Differential Relation: 1973–84, Federal Reserve Board, *International Finance Discussion Papers*, no. 268, August.

Meese, Richard and Rose, Andrew K. (1989), An Empirical Assessment of Non-linearities in Models of Exchange Rate Determination, *International Finance Discussion Papers*, no. 367, November.

—— (1990), Nonlinear, Nonparametric, Nonessential Exchange Rate Estimation, *The American Economic Review, Papers and Proceedings,* May, pp. 192–6.

Mendoza, Enrique, G. (1989), A Quantitative Investigation of the Macroeconomic Effects of Capital Controls and the Stabilization of the Balance of Trade, University of Western Ontario, Department of Economics, Research Report 8908, June.

Micossi, S. (1985), The Intervention and Financing Mechanisms of the EMS and their Role for the ECU, Banca Nazionale del Lavoro, *Quarterly Review,* December, pp. 327–45.

Micossi, Stefano and Rossi, Salvatore (1987), Controlli sui Movimenti di Capitale: Il Caso Italiano, *Giornale degli Economisti e Annali di Economia*, XLV, 1/2, pp. 2–53.

Obstfeld, Maurice (1986a), Capital Mobility in the World Economy: Theory and Measurement, in Brunner, K. and Meltzer, A. H. (eds), *The National Bureau Method, International Capital Mobility, and Other Essays,* Carnegie–Rochester Conference Series on Public Policy, no. 24.

—— (1986b), How Integrated are World Capital Markets? Some New Tests, *National Bureau of Economic Research Paper,* 2075, November.

Padoa Schioppa, T. (1985), Policy Cooperation and the EMS Experience, in Bilson, J. and Marston, M. (eds), *International Economic Policy Cooperation,* Cambridge University Press, pp. 331–55.

Radaelli, Giorgio (1988), Restrizioni e Capacita' Previsiva dei Modelli del Tasso di Cambio, chapter 4 in Avesani, R., Spinelli, F. and Tamborini, R. (eds), *Moneta e Cambi,* pp. 169–212. In English as, Testable Restrictions and the Forecasting Performance of Exchange Rate Determination Models, *Chase Manhattan Bank Working Papers in Financial Economics,* 4, London.

—— (1993), Germany: Monetary Squeeze, Fiscal Crush, Lehman Brothers occasional paper series, August.

Rogoff, K. (1984), On the Effects of Sterilized Intervention: An Analysis of Weekly Data, *Journal of Monetary Economics,* September, pp. 133–50.

—— (1985), Can Exchange Rate Predictability be Achieved without Monetary Convergence? Evidence from the EMS, *European Economic Review,* September, pp. 93–115.

Sims, Christopher A. (1972), Money, Income and Causality, *American Economic Review,* 62, 4, pp. 387–403.

Somanath, V. S. (1986), Efficient Exchange Rate Forecasts: Lagged Models Better than the Random Walk, *Journal of International Money and Finance,* 5, June, pp. 195–220.

REFERENCES

Ungerer, Horst, Evans, Owen, Mayer, Thomas and Young, Philip (1986), The European Monetary System: Recent Developments, *IMF Occasional Paper*, 48, December.

Van Wijnbergen, S. (1985), Capital Controls and the Real Exchange Rate, *CEPR Discussion Paper*, no. 89, December.

Wood, G. E. (1986), EMS Arrangements: Their Functioning and their Future, City University, Centre for Banking and International Finance, *Discussion Paper*, no. 40, April.

Wyplosz, Charles (1986), Capital Controls and Balance of Payments Crises, *Journal of International Money and Finance*, 5, pp. 167–79.

INDEX

Adams, C. 95n
Adams, D. B. 86, 89
ADF statistics 63, 65, 73
adjustments 13; external
   problems 85
agents 28, 32, 38; controls on
   39–40, 44; costs in transferring
   funds abroad 36; foreign 28;
   micro 93n; private, public
   bonds held by 18; purchases of
   foreign real estate 42; rational,
   may be risk-averse 16
aggregation problems 18
allocation of resources 6
anti-logarithms 29
appreciation 60, 61, 95n
AR(1) process 19, 37, 95n;
   residuals 23, 94n
arbitrage 36; covered/uncovered
   35, 95n; private 95n;
   unexploited inward
   opportunities 52
ARIMA models 40
Artis, M. J. 8, 27
assets 16, 17, 28, 38, 40; alternative
   financial, expected returns on
   34; currency composition of
   supplies 15; degree of
   substitutability 39, 65;
   demands 17, 39, 55, 86;
   denominated in different
   currencies 77; domestic and

foreign, interest-bearing 36;
   highly substitutable 44;
   Eurocurrency or domestic
   private banking 14; imperfect
   substitutability 26, 55, 60;
   market models 55, 56, 77; net
   domestic 86–7; perfect
   substitutability 16, 17–18, 28,
   29, 39, 40, 94n; relative supply
   of 18; which do not net out
   within one country's private
   sector 64; *see also* dollar;
   foreign assets; French franc;
   lira; outside assets
asymmetric information 35
asymptotic distribution 64
autocorrelation 19, 21, 23, 63n,
   95n; first-order problem 94n

Backus, D. 60
balance of payments 38, 39, 40,
   42, 61; equilibrium model 60;
   overall, a function of relative
   GDP and the real exchange
   rate 59; trade flows to affect
   financial markets via 60
balance sheets 87; stylized 86
Banca d'Italia 47; *Bollettino
   Economico* 54
Bank of Japan 84, 85
banks 41; allowed to make loans
   to non-residents 42; allowing

domestic households to open accounts abroad and foreign currency accounts at home 42; deposits in foreign currency 47; Eurocurrency or domestic private assets 14; monetary liabilities 86; net foreign currency debtor position 47; requirement that foreign assets and liabilities be balanced daily 47; *see also* central banks
Banque de France 41
Begg, D. K. H. 18
Belgium 15, 36
Belongia, M. T. 84, 89
Bilson, J. F. O. 57
Bini Smaghi, L. 10
Black, S. W. 22
bonds: demands for 16, 28, 55, 61, 84, 96n; domestic 17, 28–9, 55; foreign 17, 55, 96n; public 18, 29, 30, 83; short-term, allowing residents to purchase in foreign currency 47; *see also under various country names*
Booth, P. 94n
boundedness 37
Box–Pierce statistic 19
Branson, W. 55, 62, 80
Bretton Woods 13, 55
Buiter, W. H. 5
Bundesbank 32, 84, 85, 94n; *Monthly Report* 29, 53, 54

capital account 33, 38, 39; acceptable balance 44; different exchange rates for transactions 32
capital controls 3, 91, 92, 93n; balance between relative importance of foreign exchange intervention and 21; effectiveness of 31–54, 95–6nn; foreign exchange market intervention and 5–30; interest rate movements not dampened by 16; long-run ineffectiveness 92; quantifying the impact on official reserves 92; relative role overestimated 12; sign of the stringency of 12; unlikely to stabilize real exchange rates 27
capital flows/mobility 37; asymmetric effects of controls on 3, 38, 48, 52; cost of controls on outflows much greater than that on inflows 48; curbing outflows rather than inflows 95n; for the purchase of real estate subject to state authorization 42; French controls almost ineffective in checking 44; growing importance, unrelated to real trade transactions 55; high 96n; impact of controls 40; international 31, 34; intertemporal link between stocks and 36; limiting 41; potentially destabilizing 35; preventing 44; substantial 41
capital markets 1
causality tests 87–9, 97n
central banks 14, 15, 23, 26, 28; balance sheets 87; causality between net foreign assets and the exchange rate 89; EC 13; ERM 12–13, 21; foreign exchange market intervention 59, 96n; intervention 6, 84; main, trying to correct a perceived dollar overvaluation 85; monetary liabilities 86; net foreign assets 88n; offering one-way bets to foreign exchange speculators 53; purchases of foreign securities 87; typical, try to

smooth effective exchange 22;
see also Banca d'Italia; Bank of
Japan; Banque de France;
Bundesbank; Federal Reserve
System
Chase Econometrics 29
Chirac, Jacques 42
Claassen, E.-M. 41, 96n
Cochrane–Orcutt procedure 19n
Cody, B. 44
coefficients 39, 44; correlation 1n,
2n, 8; dummy 43; estimated 48,
64, 85; real exchange rate 38;
relative risk aversion 94n;
variation 7
cointegration 65, 73; borderline
77; techniques 56, 62; marginal
64; tests 64, 65, 74, 97n;
variables 56–7, 62–3, 64, 97n;
weak 77; *see also* regressions
competitiveness: changes in 85;
international 5, 6; loss of 60
conditional/unconditional
variances 7
consumer's utility function 94n
consumption 33, 34, 35
correlation: degree between
variables 8; estimating
between national rates of
savings and investment 34;
forecast error 18; interest rate
9, 33; money supplies 2, 9;
negative, between domestic
and foreign real overnight
rates of interest 1; spurious 34;
see also coefficients
costs 5–6, 95n; agent may incur,
in transferring funds abroad
36; controls 36, 38, 40, 48;
domestic grants 42–3;
marginal, of transferring
funds 36; opportunity 57;
quadratic function 36
'counterpart items' 39
credit 94n, 97n; trade 35
credit cards 96n

critical values 19n, 25n, 63n
Cumby, R. E. 18
currencies 14, 23; basket of 22;
borrowing 13, 41, 96n;
composition of asset supplies
15; crosses its threshold of
divergence 13; depreciation 60;
different, assets denominated
in 77; EMS 15; ERM 7, 13, 92;
excess volatility 3; forward
price of foreign in terms of
domestic 95n; French
companies gaining full
freedom to deal in foreign 42;
leads and lags in trade-related
foreign transactions 41; main
3, 92; markets 6, 35; money
demand shifts from one to
another 93n; dollars (and other
non-EMS currencies)
interventions in 94n; net
foreign debtor position of
banks 47; spot price of foreign
in terms of domestic 95n;
substitution effects 58; time
limits for surrendering
foreign earnings 42;
turbulence 92; units of
domestic per unit of foreign
16–17, 95n; values 84; *see also*
DM; dollar; French franc; lira;
sterling; yen
current accounts 38, 63, 81;
cumulated 59, 64; deficits 47;
different exchange rates for
transactions 32; foreign,
allowing domestic households
to open at home 42; improved
47; smaller imbalances 34
Cushman, D. B. 5

Danker, D. 96n
Datastream 53, 54, 80
default risk 15
deficits 33, 47
demand: asset 39, 55, 86; bond 16,

28, 55, 61, 84, 96n; money 57, 93n

demand functions: asset 17, 39; mean–variance optimizing 61, 84; money 58; standard bond 96n

depreciation 21; currency 60; expected rate of 60; long-run 59; real 42, 59

devaluations 19, 31, 42

discount rates 36, 37, 40–1

disturbances 13, 17, 22

DM (Deutsche Mark) 22, 89, 91; assets 61; collinearity between movements in Swiss franc and 95n; dollar undervalued against 65–6; French franc and 19, 21, 26; never unambiguously reference currency for foreign exchange market intervention 26; optimal share of German private financial wealth 61; policy advice that it should be revalued 13–14; spot rate 61; weight given to, by intervention rule of thumb 23; *see also* DMDL

DMDL (DM/dollar exchange rate) 26, 62–73 *passim*, 77, 84, 86; equilibrium explanations of 80; modelling 64, 67, 68, 69, 73, 96–7nn

dollar 15, 22, 23, 26, 89; assets 61; intervention 94n; main central banks trying to correct a perceived overvaluation 85; three-month swaps 13; trying to halt a slide 85; under attack 41; undervalued 65–6, 77

domestic interest rates 11, 16–17, 32, 41, 95n; burden of stabilizing exchange rates shifted onto 10; gap between domestic Euro-interest rates and 35; interbank 53, 54; relative 60; tightening of domestic controls and 39, 48; unnecessarily high 40; versus Eurofranc rate 11

Dominguez, K. M. 84, 86

Dooley, M. P. 96n

Dornbusch, R. 31, 57, 60

Driffill, J. 34

Driskill, R. A. 60

dual exchange market 47

Durbin–Watson statistic 19

EC (European Community) 42, 96n; central banks 13; Commission 53

ECU accounts 13

economic growth 1

economies: major 1, 2; smaller, more open 3

Edison, H. J. 83, 84, 89

Edwards, S. 31

eigenvalues 65, 74

elasticities 87; interest rate 74–7; statistically significant 84; wealth 65, 74

employment 5; full 33

Engle, R. F. 97n

equilibrium 65, 62, 63, 78, 92; estimated relationship 73; long-run 57, 66, 77, 80; money 60

ERM (exchange rate mechanism) central banks 12–13, 21; contribution to greater real exchange rate stability 7; correlation between interest rates and inflation 9; foreign exchange markets 86; high nominal and real stability among currencies 7; institutional arrangements explicitly boosting funds for intervention 12–13; monetary authorities 53; parities 92, 97n; performance and its determinants 6–14; real threat to stability 10; weaker currencies 92

errors 7, 18, 29, 35; correction models 74, 97n; level-form correction term 97n; proxy 39; standard 24n, 66, 96n

estimates/estimation 18, 23, 25n, 34, 42, 48, 77; cointegrating parameters 66; equilibrium relationship 73; instrumental variable 21; inverted bond demand equations 16; long-run model 73; offset coefficient 85; OLS 19, 64–5, 87; quasi-reduced forms 16; SUR 23

Euler equation 37, 38

Eurocurrency assets 14

Eurofranc 10–11; thinness of the market 19

Eurointerest rates 19, 29; domestic rates and 11, 27, 35, 36; Eurodeutschmark 32; Eurolira and Eurofranc 10–11, 95n

Euromarkets 12, 94n

European monetary fiscal policy mixes 12

European Monetary Cooperation Fund 13

exchange rate volatility 5–7 *passim*, 27, 33, 91; assessing with respect to bilateral rates 8; presumption that capital controls the only determinant 12; three tools with which to contain 3

exchange rates: absence of 61; actual behaviour 6, 27–8; acute pressure 53; adjustments 13; bilateral 8, 53, 54, 80, 89; causality between central bank net foreign assets and 89; causality tests between intervention and 88; commitments 3;

compensating holders for unexpected losses 10–12; determination 15, 55–81; different, for current and capital account transactions 32; dual 32, 95n; effective 22, 38, 39, 40, 41, 53, 54, 55, 89; elasticity, with respect to intervention 87; estimation of quasi-reduced forms 16; expectations 34, 84; financial and commercial 36; flexible 2; fluctuations, different means for limiting 3; Granger-cause 92; long-run, equilibrium, determinants 56; main 89, 92; major, long-run link between financial wealth and 83; market 53; nominal 5, 7, 12, 39, 40, 54; non-ERM 80; observed variability in 55; policy 84; portfolio-balance model of determination 15; semi-fixed systems 34; stability 5, 6, 8, 12, 27, 28, 34; sterilized intervention allowed to affect 18; sticky-price monetary models 1, 58; strengthened 52; stronger impact on 14; superiority of a random-walk rule in forecasting 96n; turbulence 91; two-tier regime 41; variability 10; *see also* exchange rate volatility; real exchange rates

expansionary domestic policies 47

expectations: exchange rate 34, 84; formation of 16; future course of monetary policy 15; generating rule 58; mathematical 16–17; rational 16, 17, 18, 40, 58, 96n; regressive 60

expenditure patterns home and abroad 12

exports: financing 47; illegal 47, 95n; leads and lags 47; time limit for the surrender of foreign currency 42; under/overinvoicing 35
external accounts 60
external balances 44, 52; of a country at times of crisis 35

F tests 26, 88n, 94n
Federal Reserve System 84, 85
Feldstein, M. S. 34
financial wealth 28–9, 58, 80, 83; private 61, 62, 63, 64, 73, 74, 79
fiscal policies 12, 27, 31, 33; pronounced divergence in 10
Fisher identity 58
fixed capital accumulation 33
Flood, R. P. 93n
forecasts/forecasting: errors 7, 18, 93n; longer-term 56; models 56, 77, 92; one-step-ahead 40; superiority of a random-walk rule in 96n
foreign assets 15, 17, 32, 40, 62, 81; imperfectly substitutable 16, 60; net 14, 16, 47, 61, 86–9 *passim*, 97; only proceeds from sale could be used to finance new purchases 41; perfect substitutes 16
foreign exchange 39; abolition of the record system 42; with compulsory financing of exports 47; controls 31, 32, 33, 91, 92; G3 intervention 3; laws in France and Italy 38; liberalization 32, 47, 52; one-way bets to speculators 53, 92; sterilized intervention 3; tighter ceilings on allowances for tourism 47
foreign exchange markets: closure 47; ERM 86; interventions 5–30, 59, 83–9, 94n, 96n, 97n; investors rely on

fundamental analysis 56; parity conditions on 31; sterilized intervention 34, 57, 84, 86, 87, 91, 96n
foreign goods 94n
forward cover 41, 42
France 8–10 *passim*, 18, 40 ; abrupt change in monetary policy 94n; actual versus no-controls case 46; capital controls 19, 27, 44, 45; companies gaining full freedom to deal in foreign currency 42; destination for illegal capital from 95n; deviations from parity conditions on foreign exchange markets 31; effectiveness of controls 35; exchange rate volatility among Germany, Italy and 12, 27; foreign exchange controls enforced 32; foreign exchange laws 38; foreigners investing in 95n; France–Germany regression 20; history of controls 44; importance of DM for 26; one-off six billion dollar international loan to 42; outside assets 30; quantifying the impact on official reserves of capital and foreign exchange controls 92; quantitative assessment of the stringency of controls 35–54; removal of controls 28, 32, 34, 92 ; resort to foreign exchange and capital controls 33; risk–premium equations, France–Germany 19; *see also* French franc
Frankel, J. 17, 18, 28, 55, 59, 61, 64, 84, 86, 94n, 96n, 97n
French franc 23, 89; bilateral exchange rates 53; compensating holders of assets for unexpected

exchange rate losses 10–12; depreciation 21; devaluations 19, 42; DM and lira exchange rates 26; exchange rate stronger without controls 44; foreigners could speculate by borrowing 41; nominal effective exchange rate 53; real effective exchange rate 40; risk premium 19; speculative supply to non-residents 41; upward pressure on 41; volatility of 34

Frenkel, J. A. 57

G3 countries 1–2; foreign exchange intervention 3; G5 policy coordination 93n
G7 coordination policy 85
Gaiotti, E. 85
Galy, M. 14
Gauss–Newton algorithm 95n
GDP (gross domestic product) 41; desynchronization in growth 1–2; domestic 38, 53, 54; foreign 38; public debts of more than 100% of 15; real 53, 54, 80
Germany 1–2, 8, 18, 41, 94–7nn *passim*; asset substitutability 65; asymmetric national business cycle 85; call money interest rate 63, 80; current account 81; domestic interest rates 32, 66, 95n; exchange rate volatility between France, Italy and 12, 27; foreign assets 81; foreign three-month interest rate 53, 54; France–Germany regression 20; low-inflation goal 93n; monetary convergence between France, Italy and 10; monetary discipline 93n; monetary policy influenced by that in US 66; money

supply 63, 80; outside assets 29, 48, 63–4; post-unification fiscal boost 10; public sector debt outstanding 81; real GNP 63, 80; real interest rates 63, 65, 66, 68, 70, 71, 72; reunification 13; risk–premium equations, France–Germany 19; ten-year government bond yield 63, 80; three-month interbank interest rate 81; wealth 61, 63, 65–7, 70–2 81; wholesale price index 81; *see also* DM

Giavazzi, F. 27, 34, 35, 52, 53
gifts to non-residents 42
Giovannini, A. 27, 52
Giucca, P. 85
GLS corrections 18
Gomel, G. 85
Goodhart, C. 34, 93n, 94n
Gordon, D. B. 35
Granger, C. W. J. 62, 87–9, 92, 97n
Greenwood, J. 33, 95n
Gros, D. 31, 33, 34, 36, 52, 95n

Halttunen, H. 55, 62, 80
Harvey, A. C. 95n
hedging instruments 93n
Henderson, D. W. 86, 89, 94n
Hooper, P. 55, 58–9, 60, 61
Horioka, C. 34
Huizinga, J. 18

illegally exported funds 95n
imbalances 2, 10, 34
IMF (International Monetary Fund) 5, 80; *International Financial Statistics* 29, 53, 54, 80, 87
imports: abolition of the forward cover of 41; leads and lags in 47; under/overinvoicing of 35
impulse response functions 62, 66
incomes: real 57; relative 38, 61
indices: consumer price 9n;

wholesale price 38, 81
inflation 8, 58, 93n; correlation
between interest rates and 9;
differential rates 22; fear of
importing 85; low, countries
which lack a reputation for 2;
proxy expected rates 58
INSEE, *Bulletin Mensuel de
Statistique* 30
intercepts 43, 63, 65, 73, 74
interest rates 8, 14, 47, 48, 60;
absence of 61; changing 84;
equality between domestic
and foreign 33; foreign 16, 41,
53, 54, 58, 95n; gap between
long- and short-term 58; high,
combination of capital
controls and 52; inflation and,
in ERM countries 9; long-term
57; movements not dampened
by capital controls 16; offshore
10, 32, 95n; overnight 1;
relative, elasticity on 74–7;
shocks 66; short-term 40, 59;
spread 76; three-month 53, 54;
volatility 10, 47; *see also*
domestic interest rates;
Eurointerest rates; real
interest rates
internal stability 8
intervention 5–30, 59, 96n, 97n;
asymmetric monetary base 14;
causality tests between
exchange rates and 88;
compulsory rates 13; direct
tests on 86–9, 92; diversified
13; dollars and other non-EMS
currencies 94n; earlier
evidence on 83–5; elasticity of
exchange rate with respect to
87; intertemporal trade 12;
intramarginal 13, 14–15, 91, 92,
94n; non-sterilized,
approximated by changes in
official reserves 86; relying on
the VSTFF 94n; sterilized 34,

57, 84, 86, 87, 91, 96n;
symmetric monetary base 14;
unsterilized 2, 83–4
investment 47, 95n; direct 35, 39,
41, 42, 96n; estimating
correlations between national
rates of savings and 34;
foreign bonds, abolition of a
tax on 96n; foreign, constraints
on 42; inward foreign,
deterred 52; portfolio,
divise–titre regime 41, 42
invisibles 38
Ireland 28
Isard, P. 55, 96n
Italy 8–10 *passim*, 18; actual
versus no-controls case 50;
capital controls 27, 33, 49;
destination for illegal capital
from 95n; deviations from
parity conditions on foreign
exchange markets 31; endemic
weakness of coalition
governments 48; exchange
rate volatility between
Germany, France and 12, 27;
foreign exchange controls 32,
33; foreign exchange laws 38;
foreigners investing in 95n;
impact on official reserves of
capital and foreign exchange
controls 92; importance of DM
for 26; overshoots of
intermediate targets of
monetary policy (total
domestic credit) 94n; public
debts of more than 100% of
GDP 15; quantitative
assessment of the stringency
of controls 35–54; removal of
controls 28, 32, 34, 92; *see also*
lira

Japan 1–2, 94n, 96–7nn;
asymmetric national business
cycle 85; call money interest

rate 63, 80; current account 63, 81; foreign assets 61, 62; minus US bond yields 73, 74, 79; money supply 62, 63, 80, 81; public sector debt outstanding 73, 81; real GDP 80; relative private financial wealth 73, 74, 79; ten-year government bond yield 80; three-month Treasury bill interest rate 62, 81; wholesale price index 81; *see also* yen
Johansen, S. 57, 64, 65, 66, 73, 74, 77
Johnson, Harry 33

Kenen, P. B. 84
Keynes, J. M. 60
Kimbrough, K. P. 33

labour market rigidities 33
least-squares approach *see* OLS
Levine, R. 35
liabilities 47, 86, 87
liberalization 2, 32, 42, 47, 52, 92
likelihood ratio tests 65, 73
lira 23, 26, 51, 65, 66, 89; banknotes declared inconvertible 47; bilateral exchange rates 54; compensating asset holders for unexpected exchange rate losses 10–12; crisis 47; factor supporting 96n; nominal effective exchange rate 54; pressure against 48; real effective exchange rate 55; substantial returns on assets 52; volatility of 34
logarithms 29, 94n, 96n
Longworth, D. 94n
Louvre Agreement (February (1987) 93n
LR test 65, 74

MacDonald, R. 56, 77, 96n

MacKinnon, J. 57, 63n, 64, 93n, 97n
manipulating the economy 33
market signals 85
Marshall–Lerner condition 38
Masera, S. 14
Masson, P. 55, 62, 80
Mathieson, D. J. 93n
maximization 36–7, 38
mean–variance optimization 28, 39, 61, 84
Meese, R. A. 93n, 96n
Micossi, S. 14, 15n, 44, 85, 94n
Microfit package 64
Miller, M. 5
misalignments 5; dampened 6; serious 3
Mitterrand, François 41
ML (maximum likelihood) estimates 40, 43, 64, 65, 73, 74, 95n
models 57–62; ARIMA 40; capital control 43; cointegrating 57; consumption 35; DM/dollar 64, 67, 68, 69, 73, 96–7nn; dynamic regression 97n; equilibrium 62, 63; error correction 74, 97n; forecasting 56, 77, 92; growth 95n; interest rate–exchange rate–net foreign assets 14; long-run 64; portfolio-balance 15, 17, 28, 62, 97n; two-equation 84; yen/dollar 73, 75, 76, 78, 97n; *see also* monetary models; VARs
monetary elements/factors 58; aggregates 8; bases 14, 18, 94n; integration 6; international reform 8; international system 2, 3; liabilities 86, 87; *see also* monetary models; monetary policy
monetary models 16, 17, 61, 92; fix-price 60; flexible-price 58, 59; sticky-price 1, 58, 62;

synthesis of portfolio-balance and 97n

monetary policy 27, 55, 93n; advantages of external discipline for 2; closed-economy 1; convergent 6, 8–10, 12, 26–7, 34, 91; coordinated, seen as affecting real interest rates 91; degree of freedom to decouple from exchange rate policy 84; European monetary fiscal mixes 12; expectations about the future course 15; explicit 26; French, abrupt change which accompanied the advent of the socialist government 94n; German, influenced by that in US 66; independence of 33, 39; lost independence 5–6; national, adaptations in recognition of international interdependence 9; trend towards less insular 1; ultimate means of preserving 3; unpleasant links between changes in real exchange rates, economic growth and 1; US 66, 73

money: balances denominated in different countries the only assets imperfectly substitutable in international portfolios 57; demand function 58, 93n; domestic and foreign, not the only domestic and foreign securities 15; opportunity cost 57; real demand 57; standard specification for the markets 60; variable driving demand for 2; see also money supply

money supply 61, 62, 63, 80, 81; changing 84; correlation between 2, 9; current definitions of 58; domestic 28–9; foreign, in domestic currency 28; growth, correlation between 2; interaction of demands and 57; more diverging 2; world, controlling 93n

Morton, J. 55, 58–9, 60, 61

Mundell–Fleming type of model 59

mutual loans 13

net worth 86, 87

non-banks 41

non-residents 41, 42, 43

null hypotheses 17–18, 19n, 94n; rejection of 25n

Obstfeld, M. 18, 34, 95n

OECD countries 41, 53, 54

official reserves 35, 38, 44, 48, 53, 54; boost to 40; changes in 39, 59, 86; detrimental effect on 40; quantifying the impact on exchange controls 92; strengthened rate 52

OLS (ordinary least squares) 19, 23, 64–5, 73, 87, 89

omissions 17, 35, 39

output 5

outside assets 30, 62, 64, 73, 94n; different currencies 84; financial wealth determined by 83; framework which emphasizes 80; homogeneous in the eyes of private investors 18; non-perfect substitutability 61; private sector 61; risk premia and 27, 91–2

Padoa Schioppa, T. 7

Pagano, M. 35

parity: conditions on foreign exchange 31; covered interest 35; deviations from conditions 35; see also UIP

Plaza Accord (September 1985) 85, 93n

plot of responses 70, 71, 72, 79

policy: advice that DM should be revalued 13–14; coordination 2, 3, 10, 93n; independence 10, 21–2; mix 10

portfolio-balance channel 27, 55, 83, 84, 86; affecting the risk premium 6, 16, 18, 21; elements 57, 59, 61; framework 73, 80; influences on DM/dollar and yen/dollar rates 91; model 15, 17, 62; systematic portfolio-balance 19; theory 64; two-country model 28

portfolios 35: diversification 61; divise–titre regime on investment 41, 42; international 55, 84; private sector 15; *see also* portfolio-balance channel

Portugal 28

PPP (purchasing power parity) 60; continuous-time 57; estimates 66, 77; short-term deviations from 58

prices 2; indices 9n, 38, 81; exogenous 60; flexible 58, 59; forward, of foreign currency in terms of domestic currency 95n; spot, of foreign currency in terms of domestic currency 95n; sticky 1, 58, 60, 62

profits 36

public debt 15, 61, 64, 73, 81

Radaelli, G. 10, 56, 60, 96n

random-walks 56, 77, 92

rates of return 36, 64, 73, 80; real 92

rational expectations 16, 18, 58, 96n; weak-form hypothesis 17; weakly 40

real estate purchases 35, 42

real exchange rates 7, 38, 40, 61; bilateral 12; capital controls unlikely to stabilize 27; crawling peg *vis–à–vis* a basket of currencies in order to stabilize 22; endogenous 58; long-run 58, 59; overall balance of payments a function of 59; stability 7, 12; unpleasant links between changes in monetary policies, economic growth and 1; volatility 5

real interest rates 63, 68; coordinated monetary policies seen as affecting 91; covariance across countries 33; differentials 10; domestic and foreign, negative correlation between 33

realignments 13, 21; controls biting in the wake of 35; market-induced 14; proximity of 10–11; timely 12, 34, 53, 92

regressions 18, 20, 42, 66; cointegrating 64, 67, 73, 75, 76, 77; dynamic models 97n; instrumental 19; integrating 68; post-ERM inception 25; rolling 65; standard error 96n

repatriation of funds 95n

reserves 32; *see also* official reserves

residuals 19n, 23, 63n, 94n

restrictions: cross-country 58, 60; non-linear 23

returns 37; alternative financial assets 34; discounted sum of 36; expected 34, 36, 39; marginal 33; substantial 52; *see also* rates of return

risk 18; default 15; political 35; *see also* risk aversion; risk premium

risk aversion: rational agents 16; relative, coefficient of 94n;

variability of the aggregate degree of 21
risk premium 39, 41, 51, 55, 59, 91–2; bond demands are functions of 28; determinants 15, 27; implied discrete jumps in 19; increasing function of 61; independent of the presence of capital controls 19; major burden of changes 18; negative 48; portfolio-balance related 6, 16, 18, 21; replacing UIP with 62; systematic 17; terms 48; testing for 94n
Rogoff, K. 7, 10, 17, 34, 55, 86, 93n, 94n, 96n
rolling over previous positions 36
Rose, A. K. 93n
Rossi, R. 44

Saccomanni, F. 85
savings 34, 44, 95n; wastage into public debt 33
shocks 62, 77; first-period 66; interest rate 66; real 22; supply-side 13; white-noise normally distributed 22
Sims, C. A. 87–9
simultaneity 18, 19, 21, 87
Somanath, V. S. 57
Spain 28
Spaventa, L. 34, 53
speculators/speculation 41, 92; attacks 12, 91; covered 35, 95n; one-way bets 53, 92
spot rate 60, 94n; extra variables affecting 61; future, expected 95n; solving for 59
stabilization 10, 22, 26, 27
steady state 22; convergence towards 33
sterling 26
stochastic process: matrix 65, 74; properties of the time series 62
stocks 60; intertemporal link between flows and 36
substitution/substitability 36–7, 44, 65; currency effects 58; imperfect 15, 17, 55, 60, 84; marginal rates between consumption at different dates 34; non-perfect 61; perfect 16, 17, 28, 29, 39, 40, 94n
supply: assets 18, 55, 86; domestic bonds 28–9; see also money supply
Switzerland 26; important destination for illegal capital 95n; interest rates 95n; Swiss franc 23, 95n

taxes: abolition of, on investments in foreign bonds 96n; foreign exchange purchases 47; yields created by differential treatments 32
Taylor, M. 56, 77, 96n
time: limits 42; trends 43n, 44, 64
tourism: allowances 42, 47; related transactions 41; tighter ceilings on foreign exchange allowances 47
trade: domestic securities for foreign ones 86; flows 5, 60; international 6; mounting imbalances 10
transfers 41
Treaty of Maastricht (1991) 92

UIP (uncovered interest parity) 57, 58, 60, 61, 95n; ex post 16; in the sticky-price monetary model 62; systematic deviations from 16, 59
UK (United Kingdom) 26, 41; foreign three-month interest rate 53, 54
Ungerer, H. 7
unemployment 33
unpredictability 93n
USA (United States of America)

1–2, 41, 73, 96n; asset substitutability 65; asymmetric national business cycle 85; current account 63, 81; Federal Reserve 84, 85; foreign assets 81; foreign three-month interest rate 53, 54; monetary policy 66, 73; money supply 63, 80, 81; outside assets 48; private financial wealth 62–3; public sector debt outstanding 81; real GNP 63, 80; real interest rate 63, 65, 66, 68, 70, 71, 72; ten–year government bond yield 63, 80; three-month Treasury bill interest rate 63, 80; wholesale price index 81; *see also* dollar

values: actual 19, 20, 78, 69; ADF 65; critical 19n, 25n, 63n; currency 84; equilibrium 58, 69, 77, 78; estimated 25n; external 84; fitted 19, 20; likelihood ratio test 73
Van Wijnbergen, S. 12, 27
variables 58, 96n; affecting spot rate 61; change in level of 70, 71, 72, 79; choice 37, 38; cointegrating 56–7, 62–3, 64, 97n; degree of correlation between 8; dependent 19, 40, 43n, 62, 94n; domestic monetary 22; dummy 21, 42, 47–8, 52, 97n; endogenous 18; explanatory 62, 94n; instrumental 18, 19, 21, 40; jump 10, 18, 94n; unit root tests on 63; wealth 17
VARs (vector autoregression models) 56, 57, 62, 77, 97; Johansen approach of estimating 64, 65, 66, 74
Versailles Working Group on Intervention (1982) 85
Vona, S. 10, 85
VSTFF (Very Short-Term Financing Facility) 13, 15, 94n

Wald statistic 24n
Walras's law 28
weak-currency status of the franc and the lira 33
wealth: components of 36; definition of 36; elasticity of 65, 74; omission of 17; optimizers 28; proxy 17; rate of return from 36; relative 67, 75; world 61; *see also* financial wealth
welfare 5, 31, 33; losses 3, 95n
Wood, G. E. 7
Wyplosz, C. 33, 41, 96n

yen 23, 79, 89; equilibrium explanations of 80; yen/dollar exchange rate 56, 62, 63, 75–8 *passim*, 84, 91